Doors, Windows, and Skylights

2nd Edition

Dan Ramsey

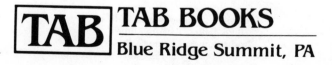

TAB BOOKS

Blue Ridge Summit, PA

This book is dedicated to the hope that you discover
The Door to Eternal Life (John 3:16).

SECOND EDITION
SECOND PRINTING

© 1990 by TAB BOOKS
First edition copyright © 1983 by TAB BOOKS
TAB BOOKS is a division of McGraw-Hill, Inc.

Library of Congress Cataloging-in-Publication Data

Ramsey, Dan, 1945-
Doors, windows, and skylights / by Dan Ramsey.
p.   cm.
Rev. ed. of: Doors, windows & skylights. c1983.
ISBN 0-8306-8248-1   ISBN 0-8306-3248-4 (pbk.)
1. Doors. 2. Windows. 3. Skylights. I. Ramsey, Dan, 1945-
Doors, windows, & skylights. II. Title.
TH2270.R35   1990
694'.6—dc20   89-49449
                                                         CIP

TAB BOOKS offers software for
sale. For information and a catalog,
please contact TAB Software Department,
Blue Ridge Summit, PA 17294-0850.

Questions regarding the content of this book
should be addressed to:

Reader Inquiry Branch
TAB BOOKS
Blue Ridge Summit, PA 17294-0214

Acquisitions Editor: Kimberly Tabor
Book Editor: Barbara Minich
Production: Katherine G. Brown
Cover photograph courtesy of Pella/Rolscreen Company

Contents

Acknowledgments

THERE ARE DOZENS OF PEOPLE AND FIRMS TO THANK FOR ASSISTANCE in researching and writing this book. They include: Jack Ulrich of the Anderson Corp.; Barbara Sevigny of The Bilco Co.; C. E. Howard of Clopay Corp.; Barbara Moss of Diston Industries, Inc.; Raymond Moholt of the Fir & Hemlock Door Association; Four Seasons Solar Products Corp.; Gordon Cellardoors; Gerald Phelan of Hager Hinge Co.; Dudley Rowe of Howmet Aluminum Corp.; Charles McKenna of International Window Corp.; Roseann Fairchild of Kirsch Co.; Bill Hachtler of Louisiana-Pacific Corp.; Susan Marvin of Marvin Windows; Nick Veronda of Mortell Co.; Naturalite, Inc.; The E. A. Nord Co.; Elizabeth Geyer of Panelfold, Inc.; Elizabeth Benn of Pease Industries, Inc.; Donald Truber of Pemko Manufacturing Co.; Janice Lee of Phifer Wire Products, Inc.; Gloria Hersch of the Pittsburgh Corning Corp.; Public Utility District of Clark County, Washington; Bob Sogge for his experiences installing his own solarium; Jon Muller and Bob Sunday of Solariums of Iowa; William Starck of Unique Window Products; U.S. Department of Agriculture, Forest Service; U.S. Department of the Army; W. R. Bruce and Lori Hajoist of Velux-America Inc.; Ventarama Skylight Corp.; Joe Kostal of Verticals Inc.; Washington State University Cooperative Extension Service; Dave Emery of Webb Manufacturing Inc.; Western Regional Agricultural Engineering Service; Western Wood Products Association; J. Warren Wynkoop of the Wynkoop Co. for Ridge Doors; and Beth Yoe for her assistance with skylights.

A special thanks goes to Sandy Wilconing for entering the manuscript on computer and to Heather Ramsey for preparing the illustrations. This book was electronically revised and edited by Ramsey & Associates from *Doors, Windows & Skylights* by Dan Ramsey.

Introduction

DOORS, WINDOWS, AND SKYLIGHTS ALLOW THE WORLD INTO YOUR HOME on your own terms. This book shows you how to design, select, purchase, build, install, finish, maintain, repair, remodel, and use all types of barriers: interior and exterior doors; garage doors; double-hung, casement, stationary, sliding, greenhouse, bay, and bow windows; clerestories; transoms; self-flashing and curb-mounted skylights; roof windows; storm doors and windows; screen doors and windows; and much, much more.

The emphasis of this book is decorating. In it you'll find dozens of practical ideas on how to increase the beauty and value of your home using doors, windows, and skylights as elements of design. You'll learn how to select units that best compliment your home's design. You'll learn how to remodel doors, windows, and skylights to fit your decorating scheme. There's a complete chapter on selecting and installing curtains, drapes, shades, blinds, and awnings to enhance the beauty and livability of your home.

There are also step-by-step instructions on how to install and increase the efficiency and beauty of basic barriers. The instructions are simple enough for the first-time do-it-yourselfer and complete enough for the full-time homebuilder. You'll even learn how to select tools, fasteners, and hardware to make your job easier.

You also get practical information and instructions on things you can do to improve the energy efficiency of basic barriers once they are installed.

There is also a comprehensive glossary to help you in decorating your home with doors, windows, skylights and solariums.

1

Basic Barriers

DOORS, WINDOWS, AND SKYLIGHTS ARE BARRIERS THAT CONTROL THE entrance and exit of someone or something. Doors are physical barriers that control the movement of people. Windows are element barriers that control the amount of light and air that moves in and out of a home. Skylights control only light. Any skylight that allows air entry is called a roof window.

Basic barriers can make a home more efficient and livable. Thousands of homeowners enlarge or replace windows to take advantage of solar energy. Doors are replaced to modernize or beautify the home. Skylights allow natural light to enter attic rooms and entryways.

DOORS

A tree limb placed in the doorway of a cave was probably the first door. The door as we know it is about 3,000 years old. Wooden planks were covered with sheets of metal on which craftsmen worked ornamental relief patterns. Doors decorated the homes of the royalty and the rich in early Palestine and Mesopotamia.

The doors of places in ancient Rome were often made of bronze, a metal alloy of copper and tin. They were built to last and weathered many storms and stormings. A few examples are still around 1,000 years later.

The most beautiful historical doors are those on Gothic cathedrals of the late twelfth century. They were often made of intricately carved wood and were mounted on wrought iron hinge plates. The Renaissance produced doors that were artistic and functional.

Fig. 1-1. Today's doors come in many designs. (COURTESY OF PEASE INDUSTRIES, INC.)

Today's doors reflect both functional—fireproof doors, automatic garage doors, and dutch doors—and artistic needs through the use of ornate designs of wood, metal, glass, and plastic (Fig. 1-1).

WINDOWS

The window is as old as the door. Ancient home builders took advantage of the mild climate of the Mediterranean by simply leaving a hole in one wall for air movement. Glass hadn't been invented yet, so they used finely perforated stone, mica, and other translucent materials to let in light and air.

The Romans were the first to place glass in window openings. The early glass was thick, blue-green in color, and contained many bubbles and impurities, but it was an improvement over other materials. Unfortunately, the glassmaking industry nearly vanished with the Roman Empire and was not revived for many centuries.

During the Middle Ages, glass windows were used in church buildings as a form of art. The average homeowner couldn't afford glass. The ones who could—castle lords—kept windows to a minimum to discourage flaming arrows and hurled stones. During the Renaissance, architects and technology offered ornate glass windows to a widening consumer market.

Today's windows combine many sciences and technologies to increase efficiency (Fig. 1-2). Special glass is used to increase the entry of the Sun's warming rays while minimizing glare. Double and even triple panes of glass reduce the amount of heat lost through windows. Special designs encourage the flow of air in and out of the home as needed.

Fig. 1-2. Doors and windows can work side by side to make a home more functional. (COURTESY OF PEASE INDUSTRIES, INC.)

SKYLIGHTS

While skylights are theoretically as old as windows, they have only became popular in the last two decades with the increased interest in energy efficiency, especially solar energy. The tepees used by the Plains Indians had a combination skylight, roof vent, and chimney, which allowed sunshine and air to enter.

Modern skylights come in dozens of designs and shapes to fit many needs and applications. Skylights are used for light, view, ventilation, solar heating, and cooling (Fig. 1-3). They are used in both residential and commercial-industrial buildings and are popular retro-fitted (added on) barriers for older homes.

Fig. 1-3. Skylights allow natural light into the home. (COURTESY OF VELUX-AMERICA INC.)

SOLARIUMS

A solarium is a solar room, also called an attached greenhouse. The purpose of the solarium is to utilize solar energy to light and warm an indoor living space. Standard glass can be used to construct solarium walls, but it is not as efficient as the solar glass available specifically for solariums. Solar glass insulates to maintain even interior temperatures and also controls the amount of sunlight that enters the home. Too much sunlight can be worse than not enough. Chapter 6 offers information on how to select and install your own solarium.

READING PLANS

Figure 1-4 illustrates common symbols used in architectural drawings and plans for windows and doors. Whether you're building your home or simply remodeling it, architectural plans should be drawn to help you visualize the end results and ensure that everything fits properly. You'll usually need a copy of these plans to file for a building or remodeling permit.

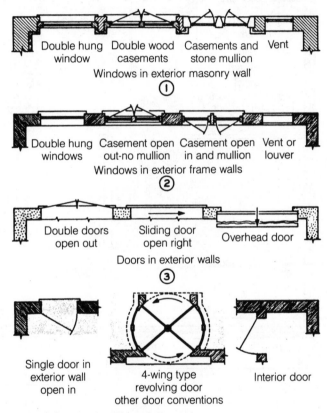

Fig. 1-4. Window, door, and wall symbols.

A floor plan is a cross-sectional view of a building (Fig. 1-5). Note that the floor plan shows the outside shape of the building; the arrangement, size, and shape of the rooms; the type of materials; and the length, thickness, and character of the building walls at a particular floor. A floor plan also includes the type, width, and location of the doors, windows, skylights, utility installations, and stairways.

A section of the building plan shows how a structure will look when cut vertically by a cutting plane. It is drawn to a large scale and shows details of a particular construction feature that cannot be given in the general drawing. The section provides information on height, materials, fastening and support systems, and concealed features (Fig. 1-6).

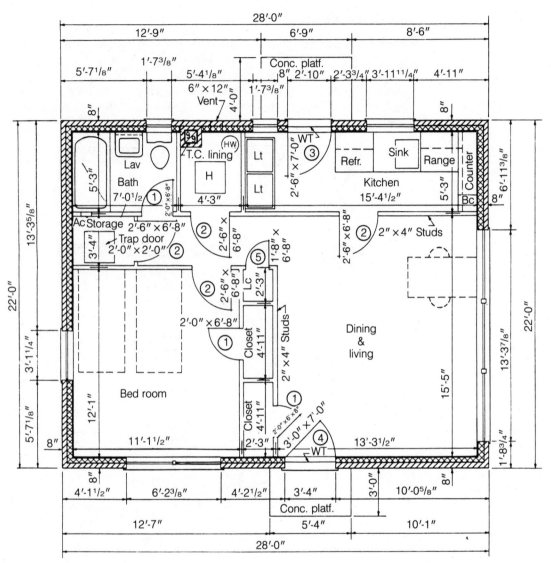

Fig. 1-5. Typical floor plan.

Details are large scale drawings. They show features that do not appear or appear on too small a scale on the plans, elevations, and sections. Details do not have a cutting-plane indication, but are simply noted by a code. The construction of doors, windows, and skylights is usually shown in detail drawings (Figs. 1-7 and 1-8).

WALL FRAMING

The requirements for wall-framing lumber are good stiffness, good nail-holding ability, freedom from warp, and ease of working. Species used may include Douglas fir, the hemlocks, southern pine, the spruces, pines, and white fir. The grades vary with species, but the third grade is commonly used for studs and plates. The second best grade is used for headers over doors and windows.

All framing lumber should be reasonably dry. Material at about 15% moisture content is desirable, with the maximum allowable around 19%. When the higher moisture content lumber is used as studs, plates, and headers, the moisture content should be lowered by exposing the lumber to the elements before applying interior trim.

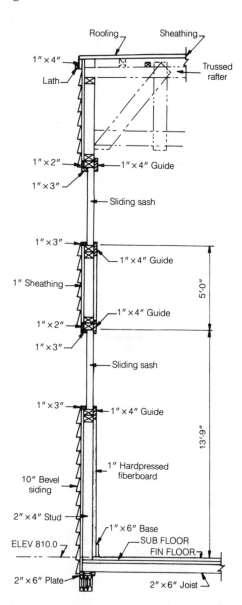

Fig. 1-6. Typical wall section.

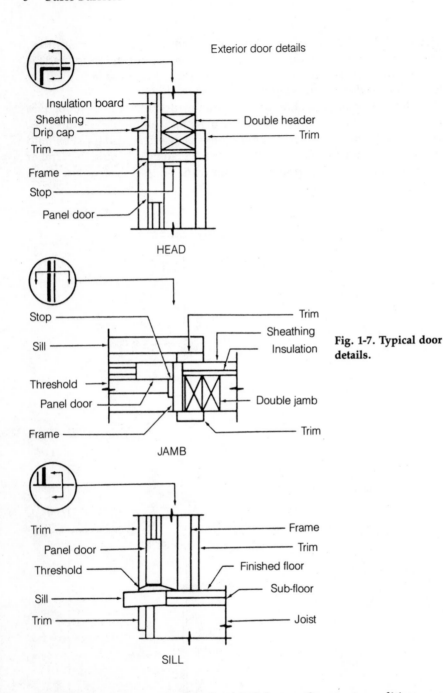

Exterior door details

Insulation board

Sheathing

Drip cap

Double header

Trim

Trim

Frame

Stop

Panel door

HEAD

Stop

Trim

Sheathing

Sill

Insulation

Threshold

Panel door

Double jamb

Frame

Trim

JAMB

Fig. 1-7. Typical door details.

Trim

Frame

Panel door

Trim

Threshold

Finished floor

Sill

Sub-floor

Trim

Joist

SILL

Ceiling height for the first floor is 8 feet under most conditions, so the wall (subfloor to top of upper plate) is typically rough-framed to a height of 8 feet 1¹/₂ inches. This allows for the use of 8-foot high drywall sheets while still providing clearance for floor and ceiling finish (Fig. 1-9).

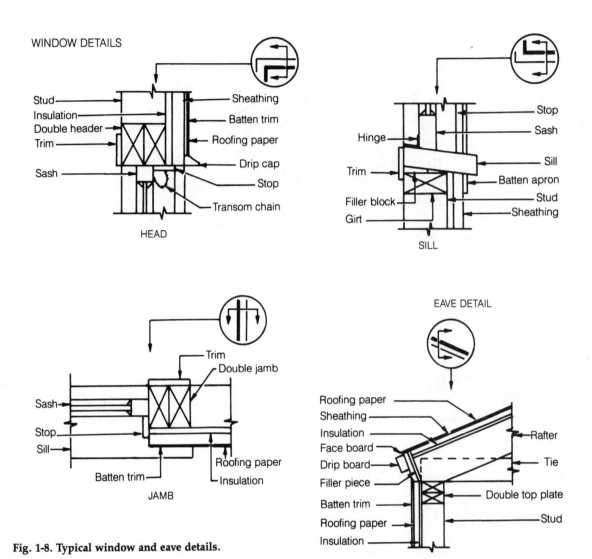

WINDOW DETAILS

Stud
Insulation
Double header
Trim
Sash

Sheathing
Batten trim
Roofing paper
Drip cap
Stop
Transom chain

HEAD

Hinge
Trim
Filler block
Girt

Stop
Sash
Sill
Batten apron
Stud
Sheathing

SILL

Sash
Stop
Sill

Trim
Double jamb
Roofing paper
Insulation

Batten trim

JAMB

EAVE DETAIL

Roofing paper
Sheathing
Insulation
Face board
Drip board
Filler piece
Batten trim
Roofing paper
Insulation

Rafter
Tie
Double top plate
Stud

Fig. 1-8. Typical window and eave details.

More specifically, the wall framing in platform construction is erected above the subfloor that extends to all edges of the building (Fig. 1-10). It is common to assemble the walls horizontally on the subfloor and then raise the wall sections into place. This system involves laying out precut studs, window and door headers, cripple (short length) studs, and windowsills. Top and sole plates are then nailed to all vertical members and adjoining studs are nailed to headers and sills.

The main difference between platform and balloon framing is at the floor lines. The balloon wall studs extend from the sill of the first floor to the top plate or end rafter of the second floor, whereas the platform-framed wall is complete for each floor. A typical wall framing using balloon construction is illustrated in Fig. 1-11.

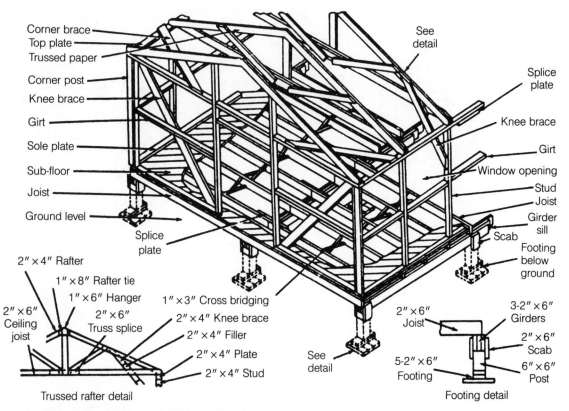

Corner brace
Top plate
Trussed paper
Corner post
Knee brace
Girt
Sole plate
Sub-floor
Joist
Ground level
Splice plate

See detail

Splice plate
Knee brace
Girt
Window opening
Stud
Joist
Girder sill
Scab
Footing below ground

2″ × 4″ Rafter
1″ × 8″ Rafter tie
1″ × 6″ Hanger
2″ × 6″ Ceiling joist
2″ × 6″ Truss splice
1″ × 3″ Cross bridging
2″ × 4″ Knee brace
2″ × 4″ Filler
2″ × 4″ Plate
2″ × 4″ Stud

Trussed rafter detail

See detail

2″ × 6″ Joist
5-2″ × 6″ Footing

3-2″ × 6″ Girders
2″ × 6″ Scab
6″ × 6″ Post

Footing detail

Fig. 1-9. View of a light-frame building substructure.

DOOR AND WINDOW FRAMING

The members used to span over window and door openings are called headers or lintels (Fig. 1-12). As the span of the opening increases, it is necessary to increase the depth of these members to support the ceiling and roof loads. A header is made up of two 2-inch members, usually spaced with 3/8-inch lath or wood strips, all of which are nailed together (Figs. 1-13 and 1-14). They are supported at the ends by the inner studs of the double-stud joint at exterior walls and interior bearing walls (Fig. 1-15). Two headers of species normally used for floor joists are usually appropriate for these openings in normal light-frame home construction. The following sizes might be used as a guide for headers.

Maximum span (feet)	Header size (inches)
3½	2 by 6
5	2 by 8
6½	2 by 10
8	2 by 12

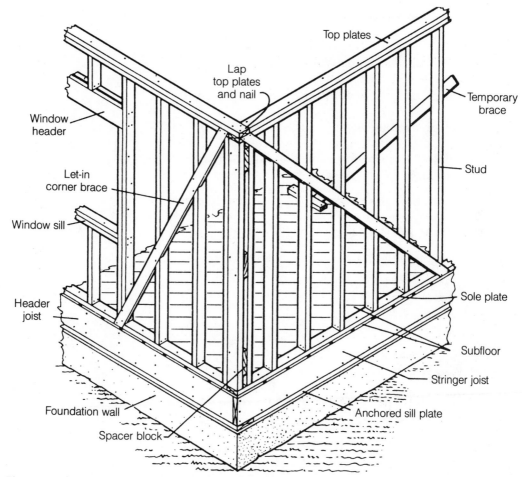

Window header

Let-in corner brace

Window sill

Header joist

Foundation wall

Spacer block

Lap top plates and nail

Top plates

Temporary brace

Stud

Sole plate

Subfloor

Stringer joist

Anchored sill plate

Fig. 1-10. Wall framing used with platform construction.

For other than normal light-frame construction, independent design may be necessary. Wider openings often require trussed headers, which may also need special design.

The location of the studs, headers, and sills around window openings should conform to the rough opening sizes recommended by the manufacturers of the door or window. The framing height to the bottom of the window and door headers should be based on the door heights, normally 6 feet 8 inches for the main floor. To allow for the thickness and clearance of the head jambs of window and door frames and the finish floor, the bottoms of the headers are usually located from 6 feet 10 inches to 6 feet 11 inches above the subfloor, depending on the type of finish floor used.

Rough opening sizes for exterior door and window frames might vary slightly between manufacturers. The following allowances should be made for the stiles and rails, thickness of jambs, and thickness and slope of the sill.

Double-Hung Window (Single Unit)

Rough opening width = glass width plus 6 inches

Rough opening height = glass height plus 10 inches

For example, the following tabulation illustrates several glass and rough opening sizes for double-hung windows.

Window glass size (each sash)		Rough frame opening	
Width	Height	Width	Height
24 by 16		30 by 42	
28 by 20		34 by 50	
32 by 24		38 by 58	
36 by 24		42 by 58	

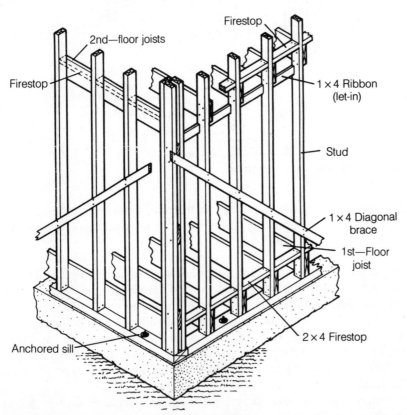

Fig. 1-11. Wall framing used in balloon construction.

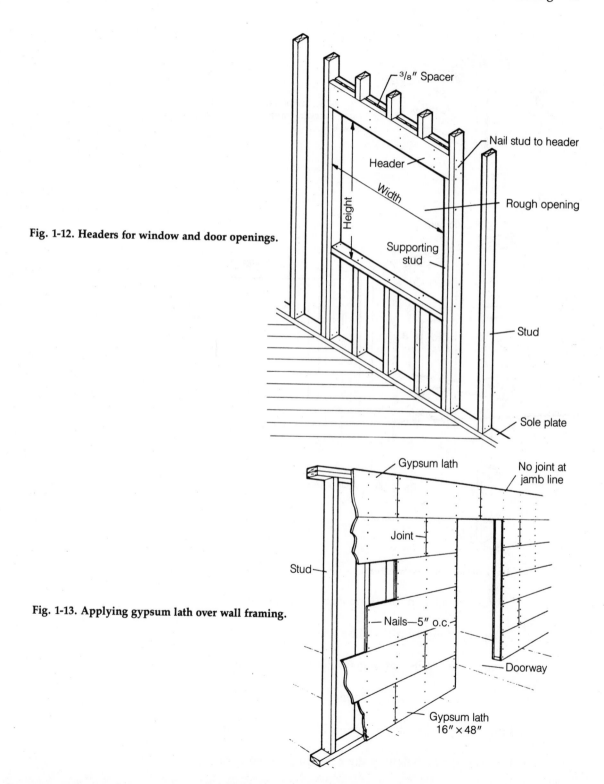

Fig. 1-12. Headers for window and door openings.

Fig. 1-13. Applying gypsum lath over wall framing.

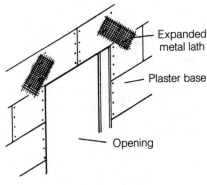

Fig. 1-14. Metal lath is used to mini-mize cracking around door and win-dow openings.

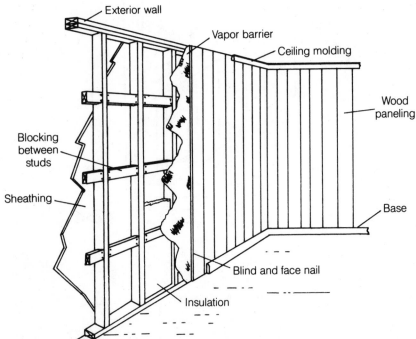

Fig. 1-15. Typical exterior wall construction.

Casement Window (One Pair-Two Sashes)

Rough opening width = glass width plus 11$^1/4$ inches

Rough opening height = glass height plus 6$^3/8$ inches

Doors

Rough opening width = door width plus 2$^1/2$ inches

Rough opening height = door height plus 3 inches

More specific figures are offered with each model of door and window you select.

ROOF FRAMING

Skylights are installed in roofs and require a basic understanding of how roofs are constructed. Many terms used in roof framing are illustrated in Fig. 1-16.

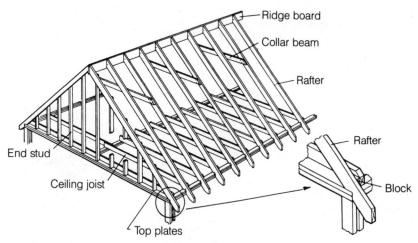

Fig. 1-16. Common terms in ceiling and roof framing.

The architectural style of a house often determines the type of roof and roof slope. A contemporary design may have a flat or slightly pitched roof, a rambler or ranch style an intermediate slope, and a cape cod a steep slope. Generally, however, the two basic types may be called flat (where roof and ceiling supports are furnished by one type of member) and pitched (where both ceiling joists and rafters or trusses are required).

The slope of the roof is generally expressed as the number of inches of vertical rise in 12 inches of horizontal run. The rise is given first: 4 in 12.

Flat or low-pitched roofs, sometimes known as shed roofs, can take a number of forms. Roof joists for flat roofs are commonly laid level or with a slight pitch, with roofing materials on top and the home's ceiling underneath. Skylights are usually simple to install in these roofs.

Three common types of pitched roofs are gable, gable with dormers (cape cod), and hip (Fig. 1-17). These are more difficult to retrofit with skylights, but the work can be done. Figure 1-18 shows shed and gable dormers. Figure 1-19 illustrates dormer framing.

In normal pitched-roof construction, the ceiling joists are nailed in place after the interior and the exterior wall framing is complete. Rafters are usually precut to length and have a proper angle cut at the ridge and

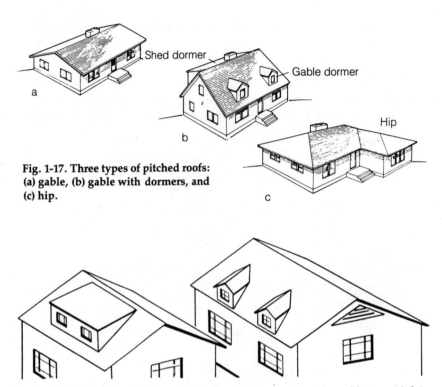

Shed dormer

Gable dormer

Hip

a

b

c

Fig. 1-17. Three types of pitched roofs: (a) gable, (b) gable with dormers, and (c) hip.

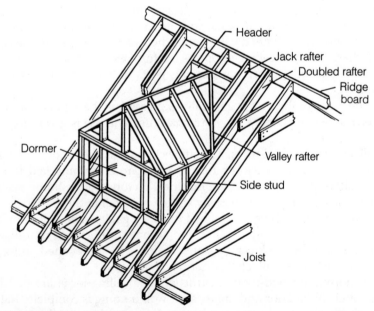

Fig. 1-18. Shed dormers (left) provide more usable space than the gable type (right).

Header

Jack rafter

Doubled rafter

Ridge board

Dormer

Valley rafter

Side stud

Joist

Fig. 1-19. Typical dormer framing.

eaves, with notches provided for the top plates (Fig. 1-20). Rafters are erected in pairs. Studs for gable-end walls are cut to fit and nailed to the end rafter and the top plate of the end-wall sole plate (Fig. 1-21). With a gable (rake) overhang, a fly rafter is used beyond the end rafter and fastened with blocking and by the sheathing.

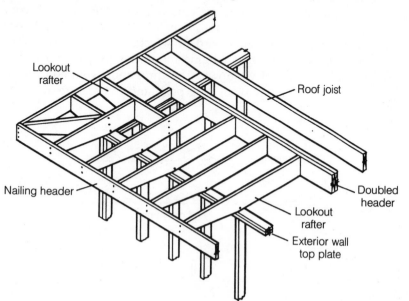

Fig. 1-20. Typical construction of flat or low-pitched roof with a side or end overhang of less than 3 feet.

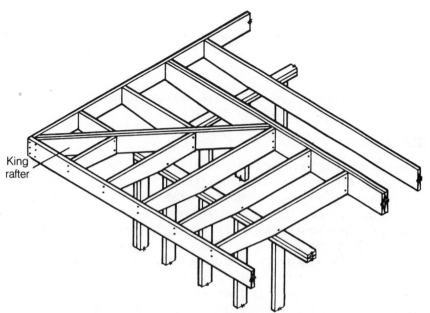

Fig. 1-21. Construction with an overhang of more than 3 feet.

Many homes today are built with prefabricated trusses. The simple truss or trussed rafter is an assembly of members that form a rigid framework of triangular shapes capable of supporting loads over long spans without intermediate support. Trusses are usually designed to span from one exterior wall to the other, a distance of 20 to 32 feet or more. Because no interior bearing walls are required, the entire house becomes one large workroom. This allows flexibility for interior planning, as partitions can be placed without regard to structural requirements. Truss spans limit the amount of roof frame modifications you can make to install skylights and roof windows. The three most common types of wood truss systems are W-type, king post, and the scissors truss (Fig. 1-22).

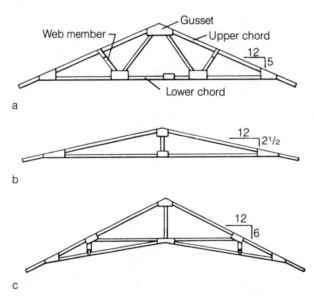

Fig. 1-22. Common wood trusses: (a) W-type, (b) king post, and (c) scissors.

HARDWARE

There are many types of hardware used in the construction, installation, and repair of doors, windows, and skylights. They include hinges, handles, catches, brackets, pulls, etc. The most common hardware type is hinges. The common hinge has two leaves that swing around a pivot. The butt hinge is most often used for hanging house doors, and it is mortised into both the door jamb and the door edge. The pin is usually removable so that the door can be dismounted easily.

Latches are used to secure doors, windows, and skylights. They come in as many varieties as there are applications. Hardware used in barrier construction and remodeling is illustrated in Figs. 1-23 through 1-28.

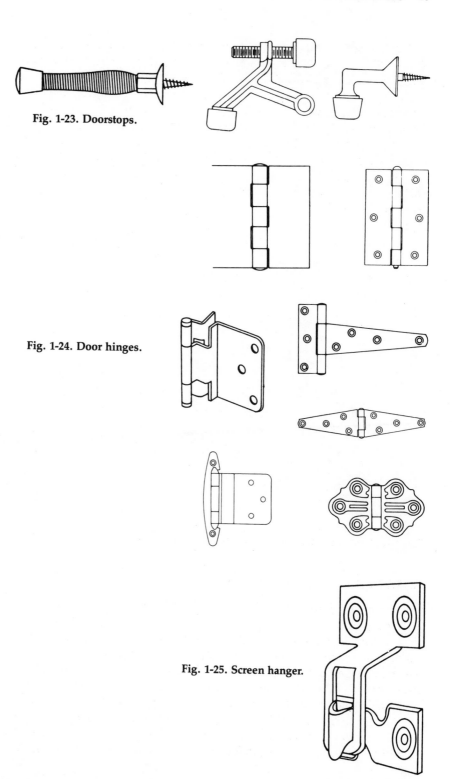

Fig. 1-23. Doorstops.

Fig. 1-24. Door hinges.

Fig. 1-25. Screen hanger.

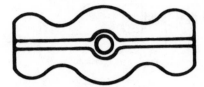

Fig. 1-26. Door "button."

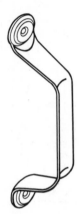

Fig. 1-27. Pull.

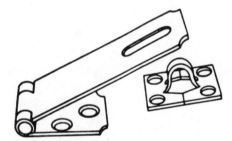

Fig. 1-28. Hasp.

2

Decorating with Barriers

DOORS, WINDOWS, SKYLIGHTS, AND SOLARIUMS CAN BE USED TO ADD color, style, lighting, and warmth to your home. This chapter describes how you can effectively decorate your home with these barriers.

WINDOW DECORATING

Windows may be covered with curtains, drapes, shades, blinds, and other items for beauty, function, or both (Fig. 2-1). Windows and patio doors can be beautified with treatments that are simple to select and install. The function of windows—keeping the outdoors out while allowing controlled air or light to enter—can be improved with treatments selected with these purposes in mind.

Until just a couple centuries ago, window hangings were regarded as utilitarian furnishings. Most were plain. A few were of patterned or painted fabric or tapestry wall hangings, though they were rarely thought of as decoration. During the eighteenth century, however, interior decorators began to focus on windows. Thomas Sheraton and other famous designers included drawings of window treatments in their influential books on interior decorating. Although fabrics were light in weight, the drapery design itself was often elaborately sculptured.

Today, decorators use fabrics with bright colors and decorative designs to dress up windows. In fact, some window treatments combine many elements—blinds, sheer curtains, and draw curtains or ornamental drapery—all at the same window.

Fig. 2-1. Curtains, drapes, shades, and blinds can add to the beauty and efficiency of doors and windows. (COURTESY OF WEBB MANUFACTURING INC.)

The three main items to consider when designing your window decorations are room style, desired formality, and color schemes. For example, a room with tall ceilings and horizontal furniture can be enhanced with vertical floor-to-ceiling curtains or draperies. Your selection will also depend on whether the room is one in which you will entertain or relax. Formal window treatments are often installed in the public part of the home while informal treatments are used to enhance the more private living areas.

The window treatment that you choose should also reflect on your personal taste and life-style. Factors to be considered include the desired visual effect, care requirements, and environmental conditions present in your area.

DECORATING IDEAS

Windows provide ventilation, let in light, and display the view (Figs. 2-2 and 2-3). You can add another dimension to the window by making it a spot of beauty. Before you decide what will best enhance your windows, consider the visual effect you want to achieve. The style you select will depend on the type of window, amount of light desired, the view, and the style of furnishings.

Fig. 2-2. Glass-block windows allow light in while maximizing privacy.

Fig. 2-3. Replaceable wooden window grilles offer decorative function.

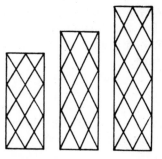

Treatments to consider may include draperies, sheer curtains, ruffled curtains, cafe curtains, and headings to coordinate with the curtains or draperies you select (Fig. 2-4).

Fig. 2-4. Both curtains and drapes decorate this bay window. (COURTESY OF MARVIN WINDOWS)

Glass curtains or sash curtains are generally made of softly gathered sheer fabric, in white or colors. Hanging directly in front of the glass, their purpose is to soften daylight and provide some privacy during the daytime. They are normally left closed.

Draw curtains or draw draperies, in a formal setting, are designed to ensure privacy in the evening, and are thus more or less opaque. Generally left open during the day, they can be drawn by hand or by cord.

Draperies, usually made of rich and heavy fabric, cannot be drawn. They are solely decorative and often elaborately swagged and ornamented with braid or fringe.

Shirred curtains, which are gathered directly onto the curtain rod and hang straight, may simply be an unadorned version of the glass curtain when they are made of plain white marquisette. In bedrooms and kitchens, however, they are popular in cheerful checks and bright floral prints.

Cafe curtains are straight curtains that hang from brass rings, which slide along a brass or wood curtain rod. Most cafe curtains are installed on the bottom half of the window only, which allows sunlight to come through the top of the window and into the room.

Priscillas are ruffled curtains that are caught with ruffled tiebacks.

They are frequently decorated at the top with a ruffled valance. Like shirred curtains, they are gathered directly onto the curtain rod. Though priscillas usually just cover the bottom of the window frame, they may also be floor-length. They may be hung so that they meet in the middle or so that they cross over each other on the upper half of the window. Most familiar in white or colored sheer fabrics such as marquisette, dimity, or dotted swiss, priscillas are also made of semi-sheer muslin and trimmed with decorative binding or eyelet-lace ruffles.

CURTAIN FABRICS

The fabrics you choose for your windows will depend on the effect you wish to achieve. Sheer curtains will filter the light to some extent and give you a feeling of privacy in the daytime (Fig. 2-5). You will be able to see out, but others will not be able to see in. Sheer fabrics ideal for this purpose include marquisette, ninon, voile, batiste, and lace. Marquisette and ninon will be the most transparent fabrics. Batiste, voile, and lace are more opaque fabrics and shut out more of the view.

Fig. 2-5. Loose-weave curtains are popular where privacy and light are important.

Because sheer fabrics must be made from small yarns, choose fabrics that contain strong fibers in order to obtain the best wearing qualities. Polyester is the most satisfactory fiber for marquisette and ninon. It has high strength and good resistance to the degrading effects of sunlight and atmospheric pollutants.

Polyester blended with cotton or rayon is frequently used in batiste and voile. This blend gives a more opaque fabric that has good wearing qualities and easy-care features.

Marquisette, ninon, batiste, voile, and lace are soft fabrics. They will look best when used as straight panels shirred on rods or pinch-pleated and hung on traverse rods. They may be used alone or under draperies.

Glass fiber is used in heavier fabrics that have an open-weave appearance. Glass fibers have good resistance to sunlight and atmospheric pollutants, but these fabrics must be laundered with care. Labels on curtains and draperies that contain glass fibers will caution you about their care.

DRAPERY FABRICS

Fabrics for draperies vary from informal types, such as homespun and denim, to formal ones such as damask and antique satin. Heavyweight, thick fabrics will shut out all light and give privacy at night without the use of additional blinds. Lighter weight fabrics may not give the same degree of privacy.

Many fabrics and fiber blends are used for drapery fabrics. Fibers that are best when used alone include cotton, acrylic, and glass fibers. Blends of the following types may also be satisfactory: cotton and rayon, cotton and polyester, rayon and polyester, and rayon and acetate. Cotton, acrylic, polyester, and glass fibers are more resistant to sunlight degradation than are rayon and acetate.

FABRIC CARE

Many fabrics on the market today are machine washable. Durable press finishes give easy-care qualities to fabrics. These finishes are most satisfactory when polyester is blended with cotton or rayon.

Dry cleaning is recommended to prevent shrinkage for fabrics of 100% rayon and blends of rayon with cotton or acetate. Glass fiber fabrics must always be hand washed because machine washing and dry cleaning will cause abrasive damage.

Atmospheric pollutants and sunlight cause degradation of fabric fibers. These pollutants are invisible and will not always be accompanied by tiny particles that cause obvious soiling. In areas where high levels of pollutants are present, more frequent washing or dry cleaning will be necessary to remove the pollutants and give longer life to the fabrics.

Dyes used in fabrics are not all equally tolerant to sunlight and atmospheric pollutants. It is difficult to predict what effect sunlight and atmospheric conditions will have on colors. Undyed fabrics or very light shades of colors may be a better choice for curtains or draperies in areas exposed to intense sunlight. Color change should be less noticeable.

Fabric manufactured for apparel purposes will not normally have the color-fast qualities required in curtains or draperies. Brightly printed percales may fade easily and thus give limited satisfaction.

Linings in draperies, either attached or separate, provide protection against sunlight damage. Linings can also provide more insulation and light control.

CURTAIN AND DRAPERY HARDWARE

The style of window hangings you choose will determine the type of hardware you will need to purchase. The selection includes cafe traverse rods, adjustable traverse rods, combination traverse and valance rods, single or double curtain rods, spring-tension cafe rods, and rods that will fit around corners (Fig. 2-6). Rods come in many decorator styles and colors.

Fig. 2-6. Decorator traverse rod with a drop-sash window. (COURTESY OF MARVIN WINDOWS)

You can choose from a wide selection of models in widths up to 25 feet in traverse styles, 12$^{1}/_{2}$ feet in cafe rods, and 10 feet in curtain rods. Extension units can be added. For special window areas, rods can be custom cut by stores that offer such services. Check local stores to determine the types of fixtures and special services available.

Decide exactly what fixtures you will use and where they will be placed—on the window frame, above the window, extending beyond the window on each side, or conforming to some special need. Good fixtures are important for they will outlast several sets of draperies and will be largely responsible for the way the fabric hangs.

When draperies are heavy or constantly opened and closed, be sure the anchorage for the fixtures is firm. If screws go into the window frame, there is usually no problem. If fixtures are attached to the wall, toggle bolts should be used. Draperies will cover such devices.

BUYING CURTAINS AND DRAPES

Draperies and curtains may be purchased ready-made, or the material may be bought by the yard. Ready-made draperies and curtains are the most popular and offer one of the best means for quickly creating very attractive window treatments. Add fringe, a colored border, tiebacks, and other decorator touches for your own special creations. If you are so inclined, you can save yourself the price of the workmanship by making them yourself.

After hardware has been selected and installed, measurements can be made. Decide on the length of your draperies. Window hangings may come to the windowsill, brush the sill lightly, or extend to the bottom of the apron, which is the piece of wood just below the sill. The most practical length for long draperies is $^{1}/_{2}$ to 1 inch above the floor or carpeting.

For ready-mades, measure from the top of the rod to the desired length. Measure the length of the rod on the wall. Stores and catalogs provide measurement charts to help in selecting appropriately sized curtains or draperies.

Although the tieback is a small part of the complete window treatment, its design should be appropriate to the style of the curtain. Certainly the ruffled tieback is as much a part of the priscilla's essential style as its ruffled valance. For pleated draperies, the most straightforward treatment is a tailored, straight-edged tieback of matching fabric.

The construction of both the tailored and the ruffled tieback is extremely simple. Small plastic rings sewn onto each end of the tieback slip over an ordinary cup hook screwed into the outside of the window frame.

You can add a subtle touch to your decorating scheme with tiebacks. Contrasting tiebacks might repeat the color of your carpets or slipcovers, or pick up one of the colors in your drapery pattern. Heavy silk cord with a tasseled knot or a fringed sash can accent velvet or brocade draperies.

Curtains and draperies should not be tied in the exact middle. Tie-backs are usually placed about a third of the way down or a third of the way up the length of the curtain or drape. You may, however, want to line them up with the windowsill or with the top of a nearby sofa to maintain a consistent horizontal line.

MAKING CURTAINS AND DRAPES

To determine the amount of fabric needed for custom-made draperies, measure the face of the window—including the ends of the end—and multiply by two for double fullness. To this figure add the number of inches allowed for four-side hems, usually 2 inches each. Add 6 inches for standard overlap. The total is the width needed for each pair of draperies. Slightly more or less width can be used by adjusting the pleat size and spacing.

Consider the width of the fabric when deciding on the number of widths for fullness. Some fabrics may be only 36 inches wide, such as chintz and some polished cottons. Others may run 40, 48, 54, or even 60 inches in width. The average is about 48 inches.

To measure for drapery length, determine the distance from the top of the rod to the bottom of the hem. Add 11 inches for hems. This will give you enough fabric for a double 3-inch hem and a generous heading to cover the top of the rod. If the fabric has a large repeat pattern that must be matched, allow one full length of the motif for each cut-fabric length required for the draperies.

Some stores will help you calculate the amount of fabric needed. Be sure you have taken measurements of the rod and the length of curtain desired.

Draperies and curtains must be cut on the true lengthwise and crosswise grain of the fabric so that when they are hung, they will fall straight from the rod in even, graceful folds. Before cutting panels, cut off or pink selvages on both edges to avoid puckers from stitching, dry cleaning, or washing.

If you want your draperies to hang in richer and more formal folds, linings will give needed weight. Linings will also give a uniform appearance to the windows from the outside. Also, some patterned fabrics lose their decorative effect when too much light filters through. Linings are usually made from sateen in white or off-white depending on the background of the drapery fabric.

OTHER WINDOW TREATMENTS

Window treatments other than curtains or draperies may be the answer to your problem. There is hardly a window of any size or shape that cannot be covered with an interesting shade. Shades are relatively inexpensive, can block out light, heat, and cold, and give privacy when needed.

You'll find a selection of textures, interesting colors, and designs that will harmonize with any decorative scheme. There are shade types and brackets to fit almost every window shape, including difficult to treat odd-shaped windows. Shades alone or combined with another window treatment offer numerous ideas.

Venetian blinds are being used in glamorous new treatments. Slats have become slimmer, and a wide variety of decorator styles is available. Colorful laminated blinds create a new mood in a room where the light must be carefully controlled. Slats can be covered with a pattern to match a wall covering or upholstery design. For large windows, vertical blinds made from lightweight aluminum and steel are appropriate.

Inside shutters can be used next to windows in place of curtains. Some are put under curtains or draperies; others are used cafe-style, either above or beneath cafe curtains. Shutters may be made of wood or metal (Fig. 2-7). Natural wood tones are often used to enhance the beauty of the shutters. The inside section may be made from any of the following materials: fabric mesh, cane, grille cloth, or screening. You can purchase shutters at your local hardware store or builder's supply outlet.

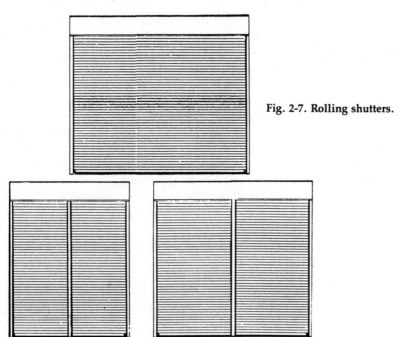

Fig. 2-7. Rolling shutters.

When a full window treatment is not desired, you may want to place a valance at the top of your window to harmonize with the decorative scheme of your room. For a kitchen window that faces the children's play area or a wooded area in which the view is important, consider a shirred ruffle hung from a regular curtain rod or a pleated valance suspended from a cafe rod. Use your imagination to create effective treatments when a decorator's touch is needed.

SOLVING PROBLEM WINDOWS

Problem windows are problems only as long as you believe they are (Fig. 2-8). You can discover many ways in which windows can be made to look taller, shorter, wider, or thinner. Their treatment can pose an interesting challenge (Fig. 2-9). You may have several windows in one wall and believe that an impossible task is at hand. Where double or triple windows are close together, you probably should treat them as one window and use a single pair of draperies.

Fig. 2-8. The half-round window mounted above a door or window allows light into a room without an interior view. (COURTESY OF WEBB MANUFACTURING INC.)

Consider using several pairs of ruffled curtains, placed side by side, to create an entire unit that covers multiple windows and connecting wall areas. Another solution may be to use one long cafe curtain to cover the lower half of the windows and a single valance at the top.

When dealing with separated windows on a wall, alternating sections of draperies and sheer curtains may be used to cover the entire wall. Place the draperies over the wall sections between windows; use the sheer curtains over the windows. This technique will give a unified appearance over the entire area.

If light and privacy are needed in the breakfast or dining room, you may want to use a cafe curtain that covers the bottom of the window and panels at the top that can be separated to admit light. Be innovative in your use of available materials to create the desired illusion.

Fig. 2-9. Draperies can be hung from above or below half-round windows. (COUR-
TESY OF MARVIN WINDOWS)

The bay window is actually three windows. The bay window must always be treated as a single unit, although this doesn't mean that you must use one curtain to cover all three windows. If you use draw draperies, a symmetrical arrangement will have a two-way traverse rod at the center window and one-way rods that open to the outside of the unit at the angled windows. For curving bow windows, you can buy a curving traverse rod and run a curtain around the entire length of the arc.

The main problem in decorating a wall of sliding glass panels is one of sheer size. If privacy is not a consideration because you live in the country or next to a sheer wall, the best treatment is no treatment. If you require privacy or light control, full-width draw draperies hung from a long traverse rod offer about the only solution. Vertical blinds are an alternative solution, depending on your decorating scheme and architecture. They should, however, be installed so that all the louvers can be drawn to one side in order to access the sliding glass panels and permit exit to the outside.

In some types of architecture, windows wrap around corners, leaving no wall space at the corner either for installing hardware or in which to fold draperies. The most straightforward solution to this problem is to mount one-way traverse rods so that the draperies meet at the corner when they are drawn and open only to one side. If there is wall space above the window on which you can install brackets, the wrap-around window offers a good opportunity to use roman shades.

If you have problems decorating a sloping clerestory, remember that it's best to leave any clerestory uncovered. The window was designed to provide natural light and its position typically doesn't present a problem of privacy. If you do want glass curtains to reduce the intensity of light admitted through a clerestory, use elbow brackets and casement curtains. Vertical blinds can also be adapted to a slanted frame.

Strip windows perform a function similar to that of the clerestory: provide light near the ceiling and ensure privacy. Strip windows usually cannot be left undecorated, however, since the plain frame surrounded by blank wall often looks stark. Cover the window with short, easily-drawn curtains or a wall of draw draperies. Woven-wood blinds that roll up from the bottom are also effective.

ENERGY-CONSERVING WINDOW TREATMENTS

The unprecedented increase in fuel costs is forcing many homeowners to look for energy efficient methods of heating and cooling their homes. Various window treatments can significantly help reduce the amount of energy used to heat and/or cool a home.

Although window treatments can be as diverse and distinctive as you wish, some treatments are more energy efficient than others. How? An energy efficient window treatment must trap air between itself and the window.

The amount of heat lost through the windows of an average home may account for from 25 to 50% of heating costs. The insulating R value of a window is very low when compared with the insulating value of the main part of a wood-framed wall. A 2-by-4 stud wall, insulated with $3^1/2$ inches of fiberglass, has an average insulating R value of from 10.5 to 13.2. A 2-by-6 stud wall with $5^1/2$ inches of fiberglass has an R value of from 16.8 to 22.4. A single pane of glass has an R value of only 0.89; a double-glazed pane 1.81; a triple-glazed pane 2.79; and a quadruple-glazed pane 3.74.

Draperies

The most common window treatment today is the pinch or french-pleated drapery. Because a drapery stands away from the wall and is not sealed at the top or sides, air leaks are inherent. The use of a valance, a common addition to the popular pinch or french-pleated drapery, does not stop air leakage because the top is open.

Recent experiments conducted at the University of Georgia and the Illinois Institute of Technology demonstrated the effect of air flow behind window coverings (draperies or shades) hung in front of window frames. The results show that when air flows behind the drapery and comes in contact with the cool window, the amount of heat lost through the window is actually increased and the air is cooled. The cooler, heavier air then falls faster and pulls in more air from the top, which creates a reverse chimney effect and allows cascading cool drafts to enter the living area (Fig. 2-10).

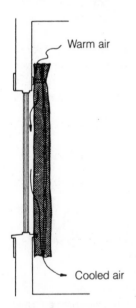

Warm air

Cooled air

Fig. 2-10. The reverse chimney effect can cause drafts.

The amount of heat lost through windows is substantially reduced when tight-fitting, closed draperies are used with a closed-top cornice board. Draperies should be sealed at the edges by securing fabric against the cornice wall or window frame. They should be pinned or sealed at the center overlap and be long enough to reach the floor or windowsill. If closed-top cornice boards are not suitable, the draperies should extend from the ceiling to the floor to avoid the cascading effect of air behind the drapery.

The Georgia experiment showed that draperies so installed on a double-glazed window reduced window heat loss by as much as 21% compared to the same window with open draperies. When draperies were unpinned at the center overlap, heat loss reduction through the window was less than 10%.

A wooden frame surrounding the window can provide the same closure effect as the cornice board and sealed edges. It may be a simple plywood frame painted, papered, or covered with fabric and suitable for contemporary interiors. Such historical wood frames are called lambrequins and fit well with many period style interiors.

Double draperies—two layers of drapery separated by an airspace—further improve the thermal performance of window treatments. Again, these need to be closed off at the top and sealed at the sides. They must also reach the floor or windowsill.

Draperies should be opened in the winter to allow sunlight to penetrate the room and warm materials and surfaces. This heat then will radiate to other interior surfaces rather than directly back to the glass. To allow maximum sunlight entry into a room, draperies should stack to either side of the window to provide a clear window opening (Fig. 2-11).

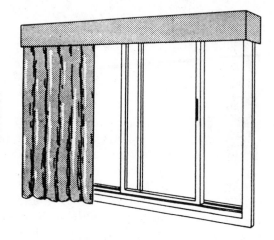

Fig. 2-11. Sliding windows and doors should have one-way draw traverse rods so draperies pull back in the same direction that the window or door opens.

Comfort is greater near windows with drawn draperies when compared to uncovered windows. This is because draperies are much closer to room temperature than the glass. This results in a corresponding reduction in the loss of body heat radiation. Heavy, tightly-woven, napped fabrics are more effective for providing this comfort. Draperies should be installed so that furnace air blows on the room side of the drapery and not between the drapery and window. When a heat register is directly below or above a window, install deflectors to divert air into the room rather than up or down the window surface.

Radiant heat gains in summer can be materially reduced by using a white drapery lining, either separate or self-backing, to reflect solar energy back to the glass (Fig. 2-12). Tests show reductions of up to 33% in summer radiant heat gains when a light-colored drapery with a white surface backing is used.

Fig. 2-12. An inexpensive curtain or drape allows heat loss. (COURTESY OF MARVIN WINDOWS)

There is a possibility of glass breakage when white linings are used with heat-absorbing glass. The glass and the way it is set should be designed to withstand the additional heat that builds up when sunlight is reflected back at the glass from the closed drapery.

Insulating Shutters

Winter heat loss through a window can be greatly reduced by covering the window opening with an insulating panel. Heat loss is reduced in proportion to the insulating value of the panel, which is measured as resistance to heat flow per inch thickness of material.

Table 2-1 lists several common, rigid insulating materials and their insulating R values. Exterior side-hinged shutters (Fig. 2-13) are available that have a 1- to 1½-inch layer of polystyrene or polyurethane sandwiched between sheets of ¼-inch exterior plywood. These units provide

Table 2-1. R Values of Insulating Panel Materials.

Material	R Value/Inch Thickness
Expanded polyurethane	6.25
Expanded polystyrene, extruded	4.00
Expanded polystyrene, molded beads	3.57
Mineral wool batt	3.33
Cork/paper bd/cork	3.40
Cork	2.24
Corrugated cardboard	2.00
Plywood	1.21
Air space (³/₄ to 3 inches)	1.00

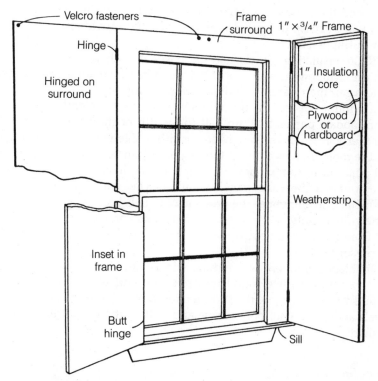

Fig. 2-13. Insulating shutters, either inset into the window frame or snugly fitted over the window, are opened during the day and closed at night to reduce heat loss and provide additional privacy.

R values of 5 to nearly 10, depending on the construction. The shutters should be opened during the day and closed at night to reduce heat loss and provide additional privacy and security. Such shutters should be equipped with hardware that allows quick and easy opening from the interior in case of fire. Shutters can also be held closed with spring-loaded screen door catches or light sheet metal brackets. Weatherstripping around the edges will trap air between the shutter and the window glass. A simpler, less costly, and more temporary technique involves placing a 1-inch urethane board between the regular window sash and storm window or even over the exterior of the window. Corrugated cardboard has some insulating value and can be used in the same manner between the regular window sash and storm window.

Insulating panels can also be installed on the inside of windows, but should be removed for short periods almost daily to prevent mildew and condensation buildup around window frames. Again, if a gap exists around the insulating panel, room air will circulate behind the panel and across the glass. This will drastically reduce the effectiveness of the panel. The panel should be weatherstripped and fit tightly to the perimeter of the window opening so room air cannot circulate between the panel and the window. A separation of the tight-fitting panel from the glass will increase the panel's effectiveness by providing an insulating layer of trapped air.

Rigid insulating panels may be covered with decorator fabrics to enhance window appearance. Cork or other insulating materials are attractive in their natural condition in many interior design schemes. In deep window openings, the window may be sufficiently recessed to accommodate panels that are half the width of the window, in which case thermal panels can be pivoted at either side without projecting out into the room. In new construction, a pocket can be incorporated into the wall adjacent to the window in which sliding insulating panels can be stored out of sight. Foam panels should be clad with sheet metal or foil. The metal skin eliminates the problem of panels becoming unsightly due to the vulnerability of unprotected foam. It also provides required protection from the toxic fumes given off by certain types of foam insulation in the presence of fire.

Insulating shutters will reduce winter heat loss, improve comfort near windows, reduce sound transmission, and provide privacy. They are bulky to store during the summer and during the day if demountable panels are used. Also, polystyrene and polyurethane shutters are easily crushed.

Roller Shades

Roller shades reduce both winter and summer heat flow through windows. A shade of any material that stops air flow will provide a reduction of up to 28% in winter heat loss through the glass, provided the shade is installed within the window frame, extends close to the top and edges of the frame, and is pulled down snugly against the windowsill (Fig. 2-14). Reflective shades, composed of aluminum foil laminated to cloth, will provide up to 53% heat loss reduction.

Installation of an opaque or translucent roller shade reflects sunshine back out the window in the summer and reduces solar heat gain. If the shade has a dark side and is reversible, it will absorb solar energy in the winter. The color and opacity of the shade greatly affect its performance. Dark-colored shades reflect very little solar heat. Instead, they absorb heat and radiate it into the room. For maximum effectiveness, the roller should be mounted within the window frame and fit snugly within the perimeter. At least one manufacturer has a magnetic edge tape on the shade that allows it to be sealed to the perimeter when an iron oxide tape is attached to the window jamb and sill. Table 2-2 indicates the performance of different types of energy efficient window shades.

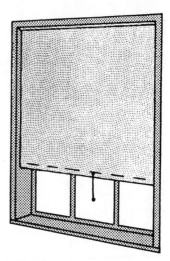

Fig. 2-14. Roller shades should fit snugly within the window frame and extend from the top to the sill to prevent air from cascading between the shade and glass.

Table 2-2. Window Shade Performance.

	Solar Energy		
Type	**Transmitted**	**Reflected %**	**Absorbed**
Light-color, translucent	25	60	15
White, opaque	0	80	20
Dark, opaque	0	12	88
Reflective transparent laminates (mylar)	43	9	48

Venetian Blinds

Venetian blinds are regaining popularity as window treatments. Besides the vertical or horizontal choices, today's venetian blinds offer other options—wide 2-inch slats, narrow 1-inch slats, or the conventional $1^{1}/_{2}$-inch slats. They come in many colors and in wood, plastic, or metal.

Either horizontal or vertical slatted blinds can be tilted to reflect a maximum amount of sunlight back out the window in the summer (Figs. 2-15 and 2-16). This action will reduce direct solar heat by 25 to 50%, depending on the color and angle of the slats. The slats also can be adjusted to block all direct sunlight and admit only diffused daylight. With a light-colored ceiling, the slats can even be tilted to reflect part of the direct sunlight up to the ceiling where it is then reflected back down to work surfaces. The amount of light transmitted to the work surface is greatly diminished in the process, but glare is eliminated.

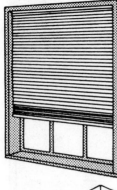

Fig. 2-15. Venetian blinds are useful for reflecting sunlight back out windows in summer and allowing it to enter during the winter. They are not tight enough to trap air behind them.

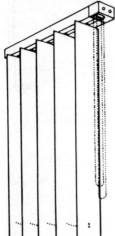

Fig. 2-16. Vertical venetian blinds.

Venetian blinds require minimal storage space when open and stack with minimal window obstruction. They are tedious to clean, however, and offer only a 6 to 7% reduction in winter heat loss due to openings between each slat.

Roll-Ups

Roll-up shades of plastic, vinyl, reed, or bamboo are excellent for filtering direct sunlight, but they admit heat in the summer and cold in the winter (Fig. 2-17). Roman or austrian shades made of tightly woven material and hung within the window frame can reduce heat loss through the glass by trapping air. The result is similar to that provided by roller shades (Figs. 2-18 and 2-19).

Fig. 2-17. Roll-up shade. (COURTESY OF LOUISIANA-PACIFIC CORP.)

Another simple treatment is a roll-up blind made of heavy cotton ducking. This treatment, well-suited for a stark, contemporary interior, offers good insulation qualities provided it seals off the window area and creates an airspace between the glass and the heavy fabric. Fabric panels inserted into the window frame are another possibility.

Regardless of the window treatment you choose, remember that an energy efficient window treatment must trap air between itself and the glass.

JAPANESE SHOJI

Translucent sliding screens, called shoji by the Japanese, are an old oriental device popular in contemporary American interiors. Shoji are traditionally made of sheets of rice paper supported by a grid of delicate wood laths. As light strikes the paper, it is diffused to create a twilight effect. Regardless of how bright the light is outside, the interior light is soft and tranquil, with no harsh glare or solid shadows common with traditional windows.

Fig. 2-18. Roman shade in wood. (COURTESY OF LOUISIANA-PACIFIC CORP.)

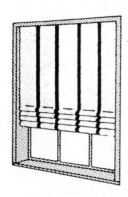

Fig. 2-19. Roman shades tightly fitted within window frames will reduce heat loss through glass by trapping air.

As the paper panes age or tear, the Japanese carefully replace them with newer, lighter-colored paper. The screen thus becomes a collage of varying shades representing different points in time. The pattern of each shoji is irregular and unique to the room of which it is a part.

To produce an impression of serenity, the proportions of the shoji are traditionally horizontal, both the screens and their panes being wider than they are high. In modern usage, however, the proportions of the screen will depend on the dimensions of the window and the length of the wall. The screen must have enough wall space to slide back and uncover the window completely. For an entire wall treatment, you may want to install fixed shoji-type screens on either side of the window.

DRAPERY HARDWARE

Some window treatments contain the hardware needed to mount them. Most treatments, such as draperies and curtains, need hardware so that they can be hung: traverse rods, hand-draws, cafe rods, etc. Most window treatment hardware comes in two types: conventional and decorative. Decorative hardware is designed to be seen and to add to the beauty of the treatment, while conventional hardware is made primarily for function.

The traverse rod is the most popular drapery hardware. It allows you to open and close the panels by simply pulling on a cord. The one-way traverse rod opens and closes the drapes from right or left, depending on which model you choose, while the two-way rod brings the drapes from each side to close in the center using an overlap. Conventional traverse rods are usually white or cream in color and, from the edge, look like a narrow letter C. Traverse rods can be stock or custom-made to mount draperies on flat walls, at corners, over bow and bay windows, and other applications. Double- and even triple-way traverse rods are also available.

Decorative traverse rods use a larger half-round rod that has decorative grooves in it and end caps, called finials, to make the treatment more beautiful. Decorative traverse rods come in many designs, colors, and types.

Curtains are normally smaller and lighter than draperies, so curtain rods are smaller than drapery rods. Curtain rods are typically full-round rods called cafe rods or tall and narrow rods.

Hooks attach the material onto the rod or clips. The two basic types of hooks are pin-on and slip-on. Pin-on hooks generally are more stable, and slip-on hooks are easier to install.

Fasteners for attaching the hardware to the wall or molding include wood screws, expansion bolts, and masonry bolts. Wood screws are used where little weight is involved and the wall behind the hardware is solid wood. Expansion bolts, also called toggle bolts, are installed on hollow walls such a gypsum board. Masonry bolts are used for installation on brick or concrete walls.

AWNINGS

Awnings offer exterior protection for your windows and can easily be installed by the do-it-yourselfer. Durable, semi-permanent awnings are made of aluminum or of plastic-coated steel or aluminum. They are available either as fixed installations or in roll-up versions.

Metal awnings do have one flaw. They tend to be rather overwhelming in appearance. Too often they are chosen for their utilitarian value only and their aesthetic considerations are ignored.

The traditional awning is the striped or plain canvas awning. They give a nostalgic look to your home while filtering light that enters the windows. Although their initial cost is low, canvas awnings do have a great many disadvantages. They are subject to fading by the Sun and rotting by rain and snow. They tear. They must be replaced fairly often. They should be raised and lowered as the Sun changes its position, and they should be removed in the fall and rehung in the spring.

Awnings are selected for both functionality and design. A local window or awning shop can guide you through the selection, sizing, installation, and care of canvas, metal, or fiberglass awnings.

3

Selecting and Installing Doors

A DOOR IS A MOVABLE BARRIER THAT IS USED TO CONTROL ENTRY INTO A home, office, building, cabinet, or other enclosed space. There are hinged exterior, garage, cellar, attic, cafe, and shower doors.

Doors, both exterior and interior, are classified as batten, panel, and flush (Figs. 3-1 and 3-2). The batten door is the most commonly used and most easily constructed type of do-it-yourself door. It can be made in several ways, including nailing diagonal boards together as two layers, with each layer at right angles to the other. This type of door is frequently used as the core for metal-sheathed fire doors. Another type of batten door is made up of vertical boards tongued and grooved or shiplapped and held rigid by two to four crosspieces or ledgers, which may or may not be diagonally braced. If two additional pieces form the sides of the door and correspond to the ledgers, they are known as the frames.

The batten door can be simply constructed from several 2 by 6 boards with ledgers and braces (Fig. 3-1a). The ledgers are nailed with their edge 6 inches from the ends of the door boards. A diagonal is placed between the ledgers, beginning at the top ledger end opposite the hinge side of the door and running to the lower ledger diagonally across the door. If it is an outside door, roofing felt is used to cover the boards on the weather side. The ledgers are nailed over the felt. Wooden laths are nailed around the edges and across the middle of the door to hold the roofing felt in place. In hanging these doors, a 1/4-inch clearance should

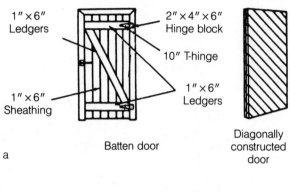

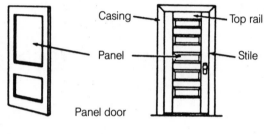

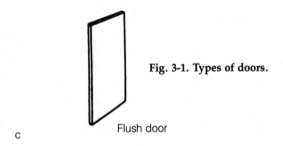

Fig. 3-1. Types of doors.

be left around the door to take care of expansion. T-strap hinges are fastened to the ledgers of the door and to the hinge blocks on the door casing or post.

FACTORY-BUILT DOORS

The typical factory-built exterior door is the panel type (Fig. 3-3). It consists of solid vertical members called stiles, solid cross members called rails, and filler panels. Factory-built interior doors are commonly of two types: the panel or the flush door (Fig. 3-2). The louvered door (Fig. 3-4) can be used as either a hinged or sliding door. Any hinged interior door should not open or swing in the direction of a natural entry or into hallways, against a blank wall, or other swinging doors.

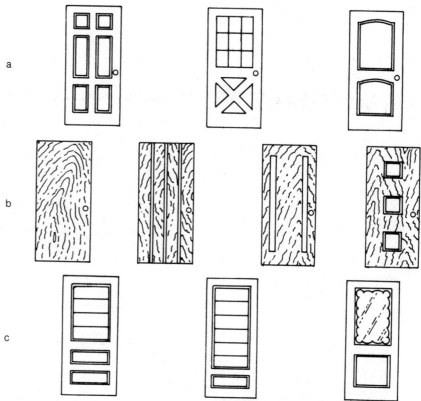

Fig. 3-2. Exterior doors: (a) traditional panel, (b) flush, and (c) combination.

Exterior doors are usually 1³/₄ inches thick. Interior doors are slightly thinner at 1³/₈ inches. Factory-built hinged doors come in standard widths of 18, 24, 28, 30, 32, 36, and 40 inches, with front doors commonly 36 inches wide. Other exterior and most interior room, stairway, and basement doors are 30 inches wide. Bathroom and closet doors should be a minimum of 24 inches wide, with larger sizes preferred. Double entry doors come in 60-, 64-, and 72-inch widths. Standard door height is 6 feet 8 inches. Optional heights include 6 feet 6 inches; 6 feet 7 inches; 7 feet 6 inches; and 8 feet. Non-hinged doors come in a wider variety of widths and sizes.

DECORATING WITH EXTERIOR DOORS

A front door should do more than keep out weather and intruders. As the focal point of the exterior, a door sums up the personality of the house and delivers a first impression of the people inside. Ideally, the door should hint at the design theme of the interior. All houses are fitted with doors of some type, but if they don't suit the spirit of the house, alteration is easy. Since decorative doors are suitable to all architectural styles, you can easily adapt your door to any design needs.

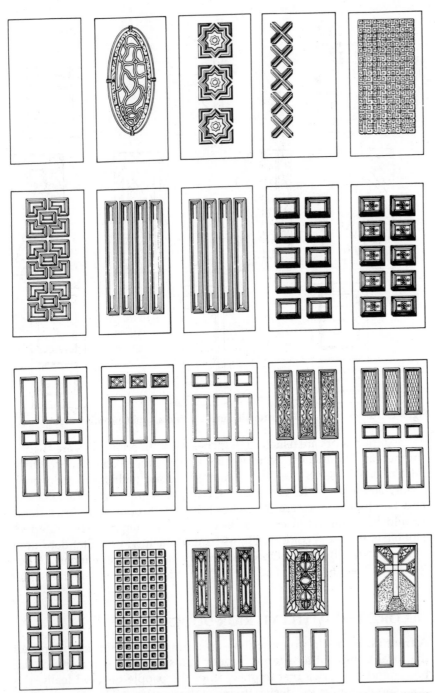

Fig. 3-3. The variety of door designs is almost endless. (COURTESY OF PEASE INDUS-TRIES, INC.)

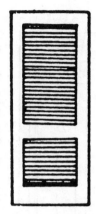

Fig. 3-4. Louvered door.

You'll see a variety of door designs in this chapter. With the right idea and a little labor, a door can be altered to match your decor and taste. Some doors lend themselves to the addition of decorative trim. Others are the result of a carefully sought-out replacement. Aside from appearance, doors have a practical function.

When rehabilitating a door, examine the functional hardware for alignment and ease of movement. Symptoms such as cramped locks and bottom sticking suggest that the door is sagging. The remedy is to tighten the screws on the hinge or, if the door is heavy, add a third hinge for extra support. Plane the bottom if the door has swelled.

Create your own door designs with precarved trim available from lumberyards. Surround a 7-by-15 inch rectangular plaque in the center of your door with 24- or 36-inch by $1^1/_2$- or $2^3/_4$-inch strips. Nail the strips on unless the door is hollow, in which case you should use wood glue. You can decorate your front door or any interior door using decorative kits available at larger building materials retailers. Another door decorating idea is to install cedar wood strips horizontally, vertically, or diagonally over the door surface and seal with a varnish.

EXTERIOR DOORS FRAMES

In typical frame construction, the door openings are prepared for the frames before the exterior covering is placed on the outside walls. To prepare the openings, square off any uneven pieces of sheathing and wrap heavy building paper around the sides and top. Because the sill must be worked into a portion of the rough flooring, no paper is put on the floor. Position the paper from a point even with the inside portion of the stud to a point about 6 inches on the sheathed walls. Tack it down with small nails.

To install the do-it-yourself door, refer to Fig. 3-5. This type requires no frame because the studs on each side of the opening act as a frame.

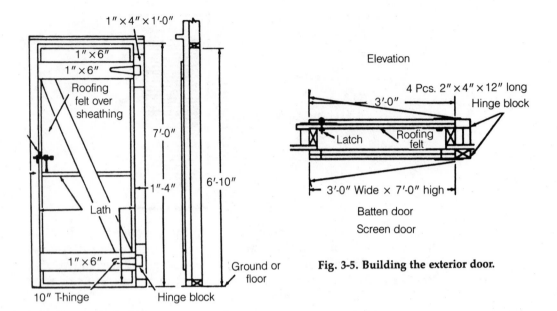

Fig. 3-5. Building the exterior door.

The outside finish is applied to the wall before the door is hung. The casing is then nailed to the sides of the opening and set back the width of the stud. A 3/4-by-3/4-inch piece is nailed over the door to support the drip cap and is also set back the width of the stud. Hinge blocks are nailed to the casing where the hinges are to be placed. The door frame is now complete and ready for the door to be hung.

The principle parts of a door frame are shown in Fig. 3-6. On an outside door, the outside casings and the sill are also considered part of the door frame. A prefabricated outside door frame, delivered to the site assembled, looks like the right-hand view in Fig. 3-6.

The starting point for door frame layout calculations is the size of the door (height, width, and thickness) as given on the plans' detail drawing (Fig. 3-7). In Fig. 3-7, the door jambs (linings of the framing of door openings) are rabbeted to a depth of 1/2 inch. The rabbet prevents the door from swinging through the frame when it is closed. Other types of frames use a strip of wood, called a stop, that is nailed to the inner faces of the jamb. The stop also serves as a basis for weatherproofing the door.

The side jambs of an entrance door are cut to the height of the door, less the depth of the head jamb rabbet (if any), plus the following:

- the diagonal thickness of the sill plus the sill bevel allowance (Fig. 3-7);
- the thickness of the threshold if above the sill;
- the thickness of the head jamb; and
- the height of the side jamb lugs (Fig. 3-7).

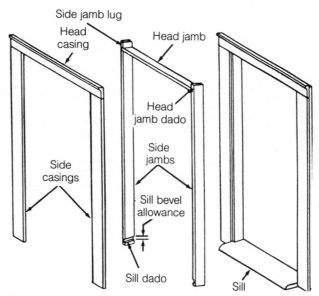

Fig. 3-6. Typical door frame parts.

The head jamb is cut to the width of the door, less the combined depths of the side jamb rabbets (if any), plus the combined depths of the head jamb dadoes or grooves (Figs. 3-7 and 3-8).

The casing layout depends on the way the side and head casings are to be joined at the corners. The casings are usually set back about 3/8 inch from the faces of the jambs.

INTERIOR DOOR FRAMES

Inside door frames, like outside frames, are constructed in several ways. Figure 3-9 illustrates the frame for a do-it-yourself interior door. It is constructed like the outside type, except no casing is used on the interior frame. Hinge blocks are nailed to the inside wall finish, where hinges are to be placed, to provide a nailing surface for the hinge flush with the door. See Figs. 3-10 through 3-17.

DOOR JAMBS

Casings and stops are nailed to the door jambs (Fig. 3-18) and the door is hung from them. Inside jambs are made of 3/4-inch stock and outside jambs are of 1³/8-inch stock. The width of the stock will vary with the thickness of the walls. Interior jambs are built up with 3/8-by-1³/8-inch stops nailed to the jamb, while outside jambs are usually rabbeted out to receive the door.

Regardless of how carefully rough openings are made, be sure to plumb the jambs and level the heads when the jambs are set.

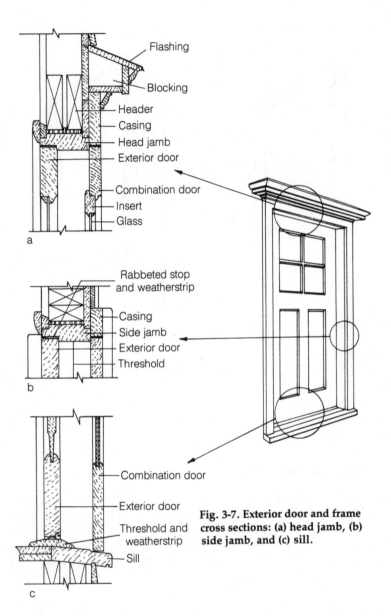

Flashing

Blocking

Header

Casing

Head jamb

Exterior door

Combination door

Insert

Glass

a

Rabbeted stop
and weatherstrip

Casing

Side jamb

Exterior door

Threshold

b

Combination door

Exterior door

Threshold and
weatherstrip

Sill

c

Fig. 3-7. Exterior door and frame
cross sections: (a) head jamb, (b)
side jamb, and (c) sill.

Rough openings are usually made 2¹/₂ inches larger each way than
the size of the door to be hung. For example, a 32-by-80-inch door would
need a rough opening of 34¹/₂-by-81¹/₂-inches. This extra space allows
for the jambs, the wedging, and the clearance space for the door to
swing.

Level the floor across the opening to determine any variation in floor
heights at the point where the jambs rest on the floor. Cut the head jamb
with both ends square, allowing for the width of the door plus the depth
of both dadoes and a full ³/₁₆ inch for door clearance.

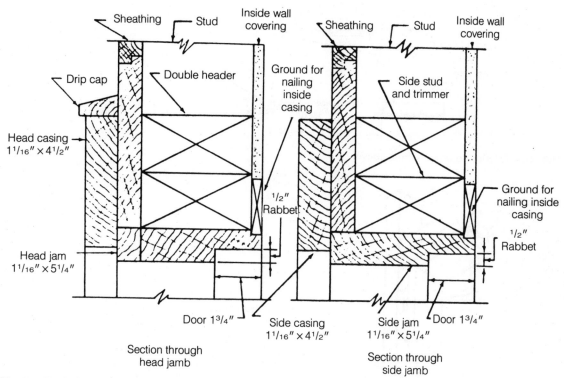

Fig. 3-8. Typical door frame detail drawings.

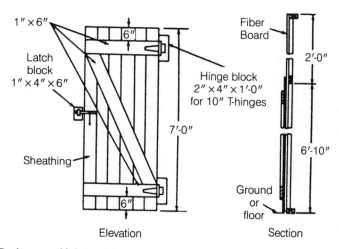

Fig. 3-9. Do-it-yourself door plans.

From the lower edge of the dado, measure a distance equal to the height of the door plus the clearance wanted under it. Mark and cut square. Do the same on the opposite jamb. Make additions or subtractions for any variation in the floor.

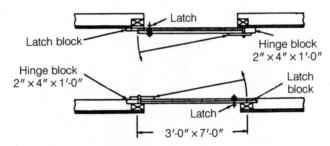

Fig. 3-10. Interior door plans from above.

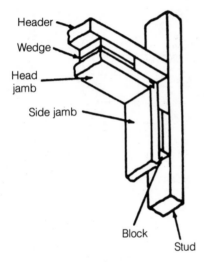

Fig. 3-11. Door frame construction details.

Nail the jambs and jamb heads together with 8-penny common nails through the dado into the head jamb. Set the jambs into the opening and place small blocks under each jamb on the subfloor just as thick as the finish floor will be. This is to allow the finish floor to go under. Plumb the jambs and level the jamb head.

Wedge the sides with shingles between the jambs and the studs. Align and then nail securely in place. Don't wedge the jamb unevenly by using a straightedge 5 or 6 feet long inside the jambs. Check jambs and head carefully because jambs placed out of plumb tend to swing the door open or shut, depending on the direction in which the jamb is out of plumb.

DOOR TRIM

Door trim is material nailed onto the jambs to provide a finish between the jambs and the plastered wall. It is the edge trim around interior door

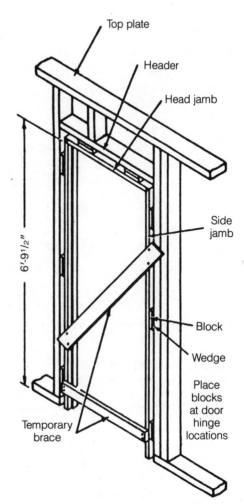

Top plate

Header

Head jamb

Side
jamb

6'-9¹/₂"

Block

Wedge

Place
blocks
at door
hinge
locations

Temporary
brace

Fig. 3-12. Temporarily brace your
door frame to ensure trueness.

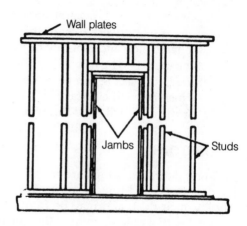

Wall plates

Fig. 3-13. Door frame parts.

Jambs

Studs

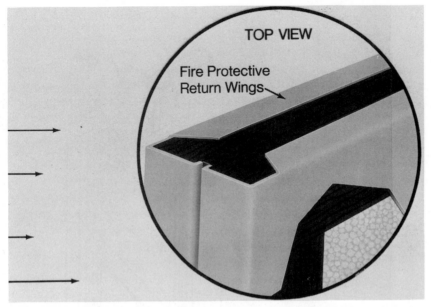

Fig. 3-14. Fire doors will need a heavier door frame. (COURTESY OF PEASE INDUSTRIES, INC.)

openings and the interior side of exterior doors and windows, frequently called casing (Fig. 3-19). Sizes vary from $1/2$ to $3/4$ inch in thickness and from $2^1/2$ to 6 inches in width. Most trim has a concave back to fit over uneven wall surfaces. In mitered (beveled edge) work, take care to make all joints clean, square, neat, and well fitted.

Here are simple instructions on casing door openings (Figs. 3-20 through 3-24). Leave a margin of $1/2$ inch from the edge of the jamb to the casing all around. Cut one of the side casings square and even at the bottom with the bottom of the jamb. Cut the top or mitered end next, allowing $1/4$ inch extra length for the margin at the top.

Nail the casing onto the jamb and even with the $1/4$-inch margin line. Start at the top and work toward the bottom. Use 4-penny finish nails along the jamb side and 6-penny or 8-penny case nails along the outer edge of the casings. The nails along the outer edge must be long enough to go through the casing and plaster and into the studs. Set all nailheads about $1/8$ inch below the surface with a nail set (see chapter 2). Apply the casing for the other side and then the head casing.

DOORSTOPS

In fitting doors, the stops are usually temporarily nailed in place until the door has been hung. Stops for doors in single-piece jambs are generally $7/16$ inch thick and may be from $3/4$ to $2^1/2$ inches wide. They are installed with a mitered joint at the junction of the side the head jambs.

Fig. 3-15. Security door frame construction. (COURTESY OF PEASE INDUSTRIES, INC.)

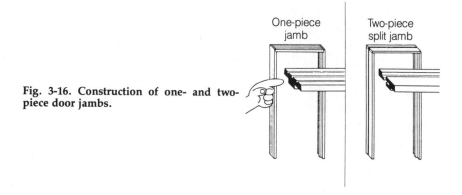

Fig. 3-16. Construction of one- and two-piece door jambs.

A 45-degree bevel cut at the bottom of the stop, about 1 to 1½ inches above the finish floor, will eliminate a dirt pocket and make cleaning or refinishing the floor easier.

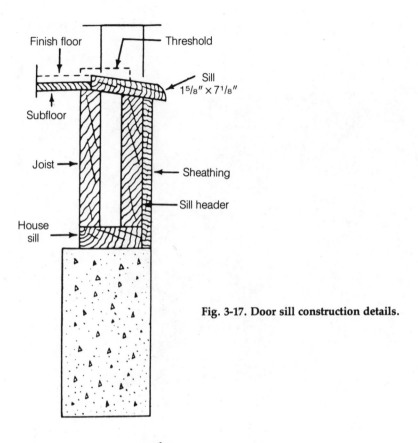

Fig. 3-17. Door sill construction details.

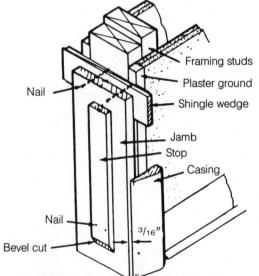

Fig. 3-18. Door casing details.

Fig. 3-19. Casing is the trim for inside and outside doors and windows.

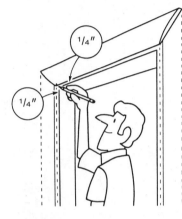

Fig. 3-20. Install the top casing first, about ¼-inch back from the inside face of the jamb.

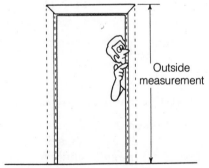

Fig. 3-21. Take the outside measurement, cut the casing, and miter the top.

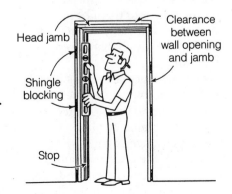

Fig. 3-22. Check the jamb and casing for plumbness.

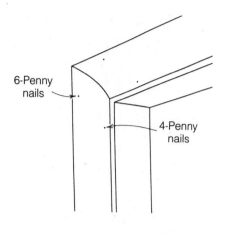

6-Penny
nails

4-Penny
nails

Fig. 3-23. Nail the casing in place.

Fig. 3-24. Set the nails below the wood surface and putty the holes.

HANGING FACTORY-BUILT DOORS

If factory-built doors are used, install them in the finished door frames. Cut off the stile extensions, if any, and place the door in the frame. Plane the edges of the stiles until the door fits tightly against the hinge side and clears the lock side of the jamb by about 1/16 inch. Be certain that the top fits squarely into the rabbeted recess and that the bottom swings free of the finished floor by about 1/2 inch. The lock stile of the door must be beveled slightly so that the edge of the style will not strike the edge of the door jamb.

After proper clearances have been made, tack the door into position in the frame and wedge the bottom (Fig. 3-25). Mark the positions of the hinges with a sharp pointed knife on the stile and on the jamb. The lower hinge must be placed slightly above the lower rail of the door and the upper hinge slightly below the top rail of the door to avoid cutting out part of the door rail tenons that are housed in the stile. Three measurements are to be marked: the location of the butt on the jamb, the location of the butt on the door, and the thickness of the butt on both jamb and door.

Fig. 3-19. Casing is the trim for inside and outside doors and windows.

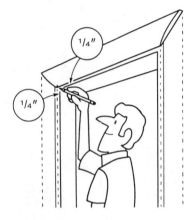

Fig. 3-20. Install the top casing first, about ¼-inch back from the inside face of the jamb.

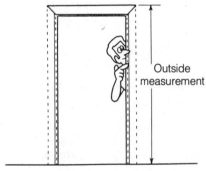

Fig. 3-21. Take the outside measurement, cut the casing, and miter the top.

Outside measurement

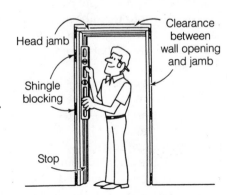

Fig. 3-22. Check the jamb and casing for plumbness.

Head jamb

Shingle blocking

Stop

Clearance between wall opening and jamb

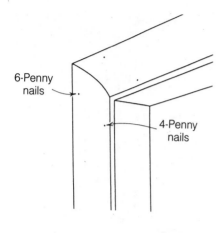

6-Penny
nails

4-Penny
nails

Fig. 3-23. Nail the casing in place.

Fig. 3-24. Set the nails below the wood surface and putty the holes.

HANGING FACTORY-BUILT DOORS

If factory-built doors are used, install them in the finished door frames. Cut off the stile extensions, if any, and place the door in the frame. Plane the edges of the stiles until the door fits tightly against the hinge side and clears the lock side of the jamb by about $1/16$ inch. Be certain that the top fits squarely into the rabbeted recess and that the bottom swings free of the finished floor by about $1/2$ inch. The lock stile of the door must be beveled slightly so that the edge of the style will not strike the edge of the door jamb.

After proper clearances have been made, tack the door into position in the frame and wedge the bottom (Fig. 3-25). Mark the positions of the hinges with a sharp pointed knife on the stile and on the jamb. The lower hinge must be placed slightly above the lower rail of the door and the upper hinge slightly below the top rail of the door to avoid cutting out part of the door rail tenons that are housed in the stile. Three measurements are to be marked: the location of the butt on the jamb, the location of the butt on the door, and the thickness of the butt on both jamb and door.

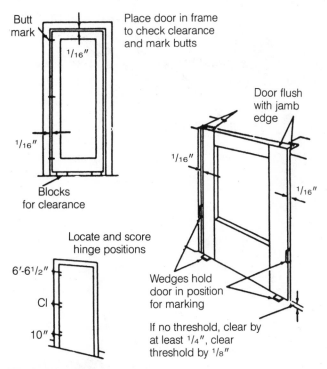

Butt mark
Place door in frame to check clearance and mark butts
1/16"
1/16"
Blocks for clearance
Door flush with jamb edge
1/16"
1/16"
Locate and score hinge positions
6'-6¹/2"
Cl
10"
Wedges hold door in position for marking
If no threshold, clear by at least ¹/4", clear threshold by ¹/8"

Fig. 3-25. Hanging the door.

Door butts or hinges are mortised into the door and frame (Fig. 3-26). Butt sizes indicate the height of each leaf and the width of the pair when open. Use three butt hinges on all full length doors to prevent warping and sagging. Place butts and mortise them accurately so the door will open and close properly and so the door, when open, will not strike the casing. The butt pin must project more than half its thickness from the casing.

Using the butt as a pattern, mark the dimensions of the butts on the door edge and the face of the jamb. Cut the marked areas, called gains, on the door jamb and door to fit the butts. Use a 1-inch chisel and mallet. Test the gains. The butts must fit snugly and exactly flush with the edge of the door and the face of the jamb.

Screw three halves of the butt joints onto the door and the other three halves onto the jamb. Place butts so that the pins are inserted from the top when the door is hung. Set the door against the frame so that the two halves of the top butt engage. Insert the top pin. Engage and insert pins in the bottom and center butts.

DECORATING WITH INTERIOR DOORS

Some architects once advocated doing away with interior doors as much as possible to create a feeling of open space. However, today many architects and homeowners prefer the privacy created by a closed door. Doors

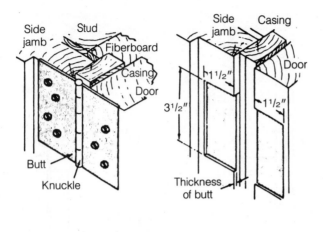

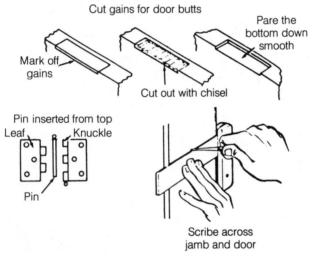

Fig. 3-26. Installing door butts.

shield personal areas by restricting space and sound. They have once more become an important element in room design.

If your furnishings are traditional, accentuate door paneling by gluing on molding. Give a custom look to a plain door by applying beveled wood blocks for a highlight-and-shadow motif. Doors on the game room or children's rooms can be decorated using bold colors, pop designs created with plastic tape, posters framed in ornate molding, or college banners. To add interest and expansion to a room, consider lighted or mirrored doors.

When planning your decor, consider the panel door, which is traditional in structure and appearance, or the flush door, which has flat surfaces over a hollow core. The sliding door, another interesting design, hangs from overhead tracks and rolls on bottom rails. This style conserves the space usually taken up by a swinging door. Folding doors are hinged in the middle to conserve space. The accordion door, a variation of the folding door, uses a multiple-fold fabric.

There are many other interior door designs that you may want to evaluate: dutch doors divide into top and bottom halves, louvered doors have slats to admit air while ensuring privacy, and french doors have multiple panels.

INSTALLING INTERIOR DOORS

Interior door frames and doors are normally installed after the finish floor is in place (Fig. 3-27).

Fig. 3-27. Interior door outside a security door. (COURTESY OF PEASE INDUSTRIES, INC.)

Rough openings in the stud walls for interior doors are usually framed out to be 3 inches more than the door height and 2^1/$_2$ inches more than the door width. This provides room for the frame and allows the door to be plumbed and leveled in the opening. Interior door frames are made up of two side jambs and a head jamb and include stop moldings on which the door closes. The most common of these jambs is the one-piece type (Fig. 3-28). Jambs may be obtained in standard 5^1/$_4$-inch widths for plaster walls and 4^5/$_8$-inch widths for walls with ^{1}/$_2$-inch drywall finish. The two- and three-piece adjustable jambs are also standard types (Fig. 3-28). Their principle advantage is that they are adaptable to a variety of wall thicknesses.

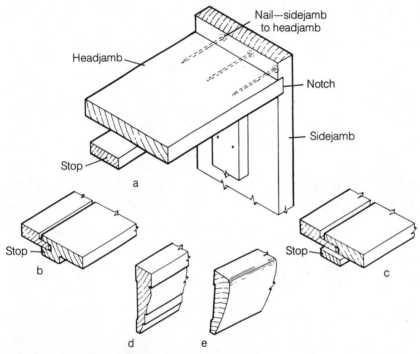

Fig. 3-28. Interior door parts: (a) door jambs and stops, (b) two-piece jamb, (c) three-piece jamb, (d) colonial casing, and (e) ranch casing.

Some manufacturers produce interior doors that are fitted and prehung in frames that are ready for installation. Application of the casing completes the job. When used with two- or three-piece jambs, casings can be installed at the factory.

Casing is the edge trim around interior door openings. It is also used to finish the room side of windows and exterior door frames. Casing usually varies in width from 2^1/$_4$ to 3^1/$_2$ inches depending on the style. Casing may be obtained in thicknesses from ^{1}/$_2$ to ^{3}/$_4$ inch, although ^{11}/$_{16}$ inch is standard in many of the narrow-line patterns. Two common patterns are shown in Figs. 3-29d and 3-29e.

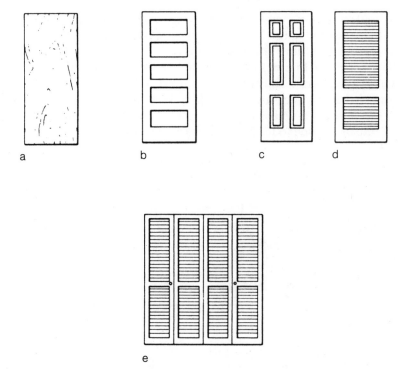

Fig. 3-29. Interior doors: (a) flush, (b) panel (five-cross), (c) panel (colonial), (d) louvered, and (e) folding (louvered).

As in exterior door styles, the two general interior types are the flush and the panel door. Novelty doors, such as the folding door unit, might be flush or louvered. Most standard interior doors are $1^3/8$ inch thick.

The flush interior door is usually made with a hollow core of light framework of some type with thin plywood or hardboard exterior (Fig. 3-29a). Plywood-faced flush doors may be obtained in gum, birch, oak, mahogany, and woods of other species, most of which are suitable for natural finish. Non-selected grades are usually painted as are hardboard-faced doors.

The interior panel door consists of solid stiles, rails, and fillers of various types. The five-cross panel and the colonial-type panel doors are perhaps the most common (Figs. 3-29b and 3-29c). The louvered door (Fig. 3-29d) is also popular and is commonly used for closets because it provides some ventilation. Large openings for wardrobes are finished with sliding or folding doors, or with flush or louvered doors (Fig. 3-29e). Such doors are usually $1^1/8$ inches thick.

INSTALLING INTERIOR DOOR FRAMES

When the frame and doors are not assembled and prefitted, the side jambs should be fabricated by nailing through the notch into the head jamb with three 8-penny coated nails (Fig. 3-30). The assembled frames are then fastened into the rough openings by shingle wedges used between the side jamb and the stud (Fig. 3-30). One jamb is plumbed and leveled using four or five sets of shingle wedges for the height of the frame. Two 8-penny finish nails are used at each wedged area, one driven so that the doorstop will cover it. The opposite side jamb is then fastened into place with shingle wedges and finishing nails, using the first jamb as a guide to keeping a uniform width.

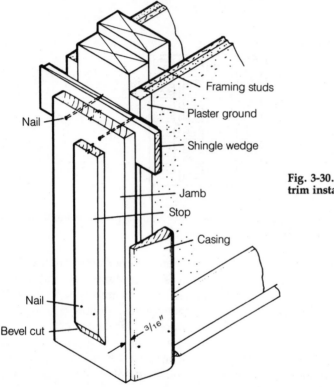

Framing studs

Plaster ground

Nail

Shingle wedge

Fig. 3-30. Door frame and trim installation.

Jamb

Stop

Casing

Nail

Bevel cut

3\16"

Casings are nailed in both the jamb and the framing studs or header. Allow about a 3/16-inch edge distance from the face of the jamb. Finish or casing nails are then used to nail into the stud. Four-penny finishing nails or 1 1/2-inch brads are used to fasten the thinner edge of the casing to the jamb. With hardwood, it is usually advisable to predrill to prevent splitting. Nails in the casing are placed in pairs (Fig. 3-31) and spaced about 16 inches apart along the full height of the opening and at the head jamb.

Casing with any form of molded shape must have a mitered joint at the corners (Fig. 3-31). When casing is square-edged, a butt joint may be made at the junction of the side and head casing (Fig. 3-31). If the moisture content of the casing is high, a mitered joint may open slightly at the

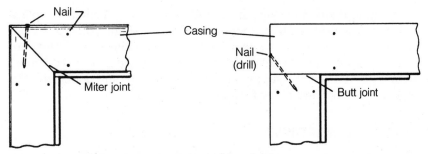

Fig. 3-31. Door trim casing: miter joint and butt joint.

outer edge as the material dries. This can be minimized by using a small glued spline at the corner of the mitered joint. Use of a spline joint under any moisture condition is considered good practice. Some prefitted door jamb and casing units are provided with splined joints. Nailing into the joint after drilling will aid in retaining a close fit (Fig. 3-31).

The door opening is now complete except for fitting and securing the hardware and nailing the stops in proper position. Interior doors are normally hung with two 3½-by-3½-inch loose pin butt hinges. The door is fitted into the opening with clearances shown in Fig. 3-32.

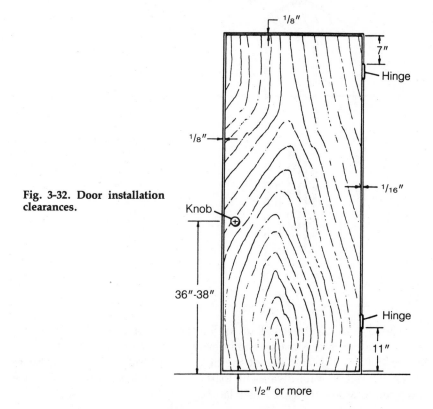

Fig. 3-32. Door installation clearances.

In fitting doors, the stops are usually temporarily nailed into place until the door has been hung. Stops for doors in single-piece jambs are generally $7/16$-inch thick and may be $3/4$ to $2^1/4$ inches wide. They are installed with a mitered joint at the junction of the side and head jambs.

Some manufacturers supply prefitted door jambs and doors with the hinge slots routed and ready for simple installation.

INSTALLING HARDWARE

To keep the door closed, you need to install a lockset, a strike plate, and the doorstops. Types of door locksets differ with regard to installation, initial cost, and the amount of labor needed to set them. Locksets are usually supplied with instructions on how to install them. Some types require that the edge and face of the door be drilled and the edge routed to accommodate the lockset and faceplate (Fig. 3-33). A more common bored-type (Fig. 3-34) is much easier to install. It requires only one hole to be drilled in the edge and one in the face of the door. Boring jigs and faceplate markers are available to provide accurate installation.

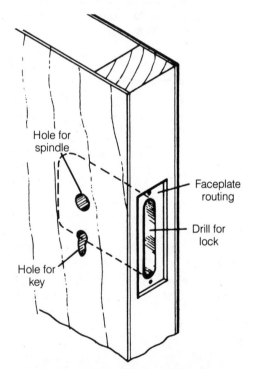

Hole for spindle

Faceplate routing

Drill for lock

Hole for key

Fig. 3-33. Installing mortise locks.

The lock should be installed so that the doorknob is 36 to 38 inches above the floor line. Most sets come with proper templates marking the location of the lock and size of the holes to be drilled. Many hardware stores that sell door hardware will loan or rent you large drill bits that are designed to assist in lockset installation.

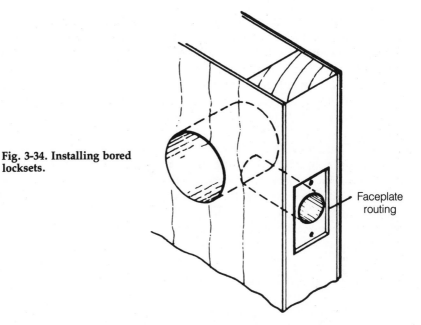

Fig. 3-34. Installing bored locksets.

Faceplate routing

The strike plate, which is routed into the door jamb, holds the door in place through contact with the latch. To install, mark the location of the latch on the door jamb and locate the strike plate. Rout out the marked outline with a chisel. Also rout for the latch (Fig. 3-35). The strike plate should be flush with or slightly below the face of the door jamb. When the door is latched, its face should be flush with the edge of the jamb.

The stops that were set temporarily during the fitting of the door and the installation of the hardware may now be nailed into place permanently (Fig. 3-36). Finish nails or brads, $1^{1}/_{2}$ inches long, should be used. The stop on the lock side should be nailed first, setting it tight against the door face when the door is latched. Space the nails 16 inches apart in pairs.

The stop behind the hinge side is nailed next. A $^{1}/_{32}$-inch clearance from the door face should be allowed (Fig. 3-32) to prevent the door from scraping when it is opened. The head jamb stop is then nailed in place. Remember that when the door and trim are painted, some of the clearances will be taken up.

REPLACING A DOOR

Often, only the door needs to be replaced (Figs. 3-37 through 3-45). To protect your finish wall and trim, run a razor blade around the perimeter of the trim before you remove it. This will give you a clean break from your paint or wallpaper. Then carefully remove the interior door trim and save it.

Next, remove the existing hinge pins and then remove the old door from the opening and set it aside. Remove the screws and hinge plates, the existing lock strike plate, weatherstripping, and threshold. Make sure that the opening is square and the sill is level.

Position the replacement door in the opening. Do not cut the shipping bands as they keep the unit square and aid in installation. Use a pencil or masking tape to mark the location of the door sill on your floor. Lift the door unit back out of the opening. Measure 3 3/4 inches from the interior sill guideline and mark the exterior sill guideline, parallel to the first. This guideline will aid in the placement of caulking beads.

Sweep away surface dirt from the sill area and carefully apply two beads of caulk. Be sure to bring caulk about 1 inch inside the interior scribed line and about 1/2 inch inside the exterior scribed line. Caulk completely around the sides of the jambs.

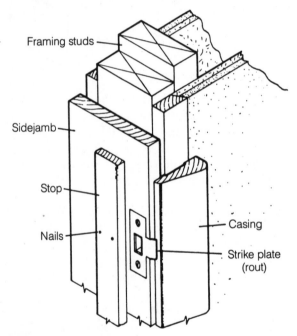

Fig. 3-35. Installing the strike plate.

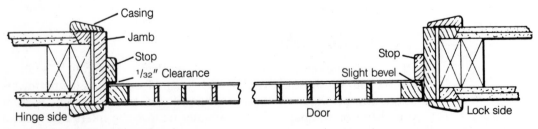

Fig. 3-36. Installing doorstops.

Fig. 3-37. Measure the width of the doorway in several places. (COURTESY OF FIR & HEMLOCK DOOR ASSOCIATION)

Shim between the old jamb and the lock area on the replacement door's frame with a ¹/₄-inch lath stock to prevent forced entry from spreading the jambs. Put the replacement door in the opening. Don't smear beads of caulk. The unit should be shifted slightly to the lock side for security.

Use a level to make sure that the hinge side of the unit is plumb to the face of the wall in the opening. Nail through six predrilled holes on the hinge side of the metal flange. Don't set nails in slots yet.

Adjust the lock side of the frame in or out until it is flush with the opening. Use a level to check that the lock side is plumb. Shim as necessary. Nail through the six predrilled holes in the lock side of the metal flange. Cut and remove shipping bands from the replacement door.

Fig. 3-38. Measure the door jamb, allowing room at the bottom for the sill or carpet. No more than ³/₄ inch should be trimmed from the width with a maximum of ³/₈ inch from each side. (COURTESY OF FIR & HEMLOCK DOOR ASSOCIATION)

Drill three ¹/₈-inch pilot holes through the jamb and into the stud (one at each hinge). Install screws, torqueing them down until the heads are flush with the hinge surface. Do not screw them in too tight or the frame will be distorted.

Check to make sure the head margin is even and correct. Open and close the door to check for smooth operation. If it rubs or binds on the frame, straighten the top hinge screw a bit. When the door operates smoothly, secure the frame.

For the lockset, drill two ¹/₈-inch pilot holes through predrilled holes in the lock frame. Torque screws down until the heads are flush with the lock frame. Open and close the door to make sure it meets the lock frame properly. Make adjustments as needed.

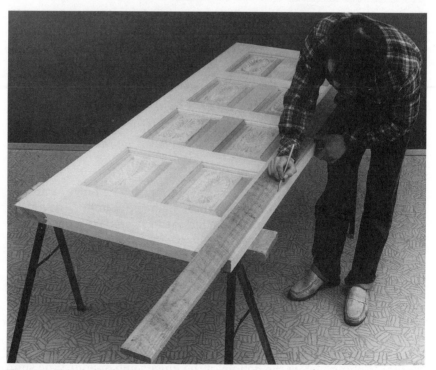

Fig. 3-40. Take half of the required trim off each side of the door. (COURTESY OF FIR & HEMLOCK DOOR ASSOCIATION)

Fig. 3-41. Larger trims can be done with a circular saw. (COURTESY OF FIR & HEMLOCK DOOR ASSOCIATION)

Replacement doors and hardware can be found at most larger hardware and building material outlets.

CORRECTING INSTALLATION PROBLEMS

If properly installed, interior and exterior doors will give you many years of trouble-free performance. Here are some of the more common installation problems and how to correct them.

Door doesn't make contact. Frame is wracked. The hinge jamb and lock jamb are not in the same vertical plane. Solution: drive nails through the lock jamb and correctly align the lock jamb with the door so that the weatherstripping meets the door evenly. If the wracking is less than 1/8 inch, weatherstripping can be adjusted out to meet the door.

Side jamb uneven. Solution: shim the lock jamb until the margin between the door and jamb is even from top to bottom. The margin should be about the thickness of a 50-cent piece.

Head jamb too wide. Unit is not square; bolt and strike are misaligned. Solution: shim the bottom of the hinge jamb or adjust the shim behind the top hinge.

Fig. 3-42. Smaller trims should be done with a wood plane. (COURTESY OF FIR & HEM-LOCK DOOR ASSOCIATION)

Side jamb margin too wide from top hinge. The weight of the door has caused a bow in the jamb above the top hinge and below the bottom hinge. Solution: use long screws in the top hinge to pull the door to the hinge jamb. An additional shim also may be required at the bottom hinge. Both of these corrections will help to restore the proper margin on all four sides of the door unit.

GARAGE DOORS

The two overhead garage doors most commonly used are the single-section swing and the sectional type (Figs. 3-46 and 3-47). The swing door is hung with side and overhead brackets on an overhead track. The door must be pulled outward slightly at the bottom as it is opened. The sectional type, in four or five horizontal hinged sections, has a similar track,

Fig. 3-43. Cutting hinge insets. (COURTESY OF FIR & HEMLOCK DOOR ASSOCIATION)

which extends along the sides and under the ceiling framing, with a roller for the side of each section. It is opened by lifting and is adaptable to automatic, electrical opening with remote control devices. The standard desirable size for a single door is 9 feet in width by 6 1/2 or 7 feet in height. Double doors are usually 16 by 6 1/2 or 7 feet in size.

Garage doors vary in design, but those most often used are the panel type with solid stiles and rails and panel fillers. A glazed panel section is often included. The clearance required above the top of the door is usually about 12 inches. Low-headroom brackets are available when such clearance is not possible.

The header beam over garage doors should be designed for the snow load that might be imposed on the roof above. In wide openings, this may be a steel I beam or a built-up wood section. For spans of 8 or 9 feet,

Fig. 3-44. Hanging the new door. (COURTESY OF FIR & HEMLOCK DOOR ASSOCIATION)

two doubled 2 by 10s of high-grade Douglas fir or similar species are commonly used when only snow loads must be considered. If floor loads are also imposed on the header, a steel I beam or wide-flange beam is usually selected.

Installing a Garage Door

Garage doors are very easy to install. Because sectional garage doors are the largest and most popular, I'll illustrate basic garage door installation with this type. Directions can easily be modified for the swing type.

The tools you will need to install or replace a garage door are a step-ladder, drill, screwdriver, level, wrenches, and hammer.

Fig. 3-45. Steps in installing the replacement door: caulk the sill area and put the door into the opening with one installer outside and one inside; shim the door on the top and hinge side; nail the hinge-side frame to the wall stud temporarily, then remove the shipping braces; finally, adjust the lock side of the door frame in or out as needed and nail the unit permanently.

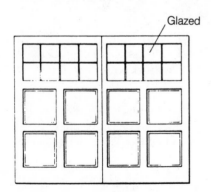

Fig. 3-46. One-section swing garage door.

Before you begin your installation, measure the door opening (Fig. 3-48). Measure both opening height and width in feet and inches. Remember that you need at least 12 inches headroom and 3 inches side-room around the opening for the tracks.

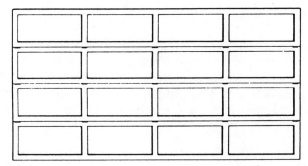

Fig. 3-47. Sectional garage door.

Fig. 3-48. Sizing a garage door.

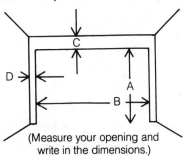

Here's how you measure for the right size door:

(Measure your opening and write in the dimensions.)

A. Door opening height _____ ft. _____ in.
B. Door opening width _____ ft. _____ in.

"Be sure to have at least 10″ for single doors and 12″ for double doors (C), and at least 4″ of sideroom (D)." (Headroom is that space from the door opening header to an overhead structure. Sideroom is that space from the side of the opening to the wall.)

If you must first remove the old door, make sure the door is down and locked. Don't remove more than one hinge, roller, or top roller carrier at the same time. If you plan to use the old door again, run a diagonal chalk line down the back side so that panels can later be matched before reinstallation.

Check the door opening to make sure it is square. If not, shim or replace side and head jambs as needed.

When your garage door is purchased and delivered, pull out all the instructions and the parts list. Check over each item to make sure everything you need is there.

Stack the sections in the opening, starting with the bottom section. Make simple shims and level the bottom section. As long as the first section is level, the entire door will be true. Assemble and mount the vertical track to the wall. Place the vertical track over the rollers. Make sure that the vertical tracks are level. Fasten the track brackets temporarily to the wall.

The next step is to mount the horizontal track to the ceiling. After you determine that the horizontal overhead track is square with the opening, fasten the track hangers and/or braces. Tighten all brackets and fasteners (Figs. 3-49 and 3-50). Install the tension springs. Adjust the springs after painting and glazing, which add extra weight, are completed.

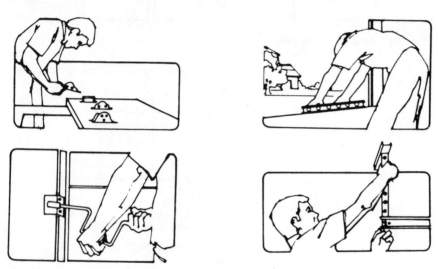

Fig. 3-49. Installing the garage door: place brackets on sections, mount rollers, install roller tracks, and mount back hangers.

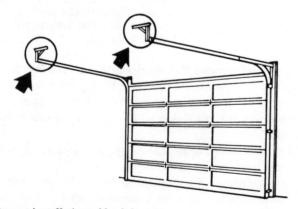

Fig. 3-50. Correct installation of back hangers.

Maintaining a Garage Door

Manufacturers of garage doors suggest that you regularly inspect your unit to ensure many years of trouble-free service.

Every six months you should inspect cables and springs for excessive wear and lubricate areas of the door molding that come in contact with the door using wax or a silicone lubricant.

Every 12 months you will need to lubricate and inspect rollers, torsion-spring shaft-bearing brackets, and pulleys; make sure bolts and screw fasteners are tightly secured; lubricate the lock cylinder with a graphite lubricant; and inspect window glazing and the top, bottom, and edges of the wooden doors. Be sure the door is sealed from the weather.

Figure 3-51 illustrates the most common parts that need replacement on sectional garage doors: extension springs, the spring pulley, the lifting cable, the bracket, and the bottom roller. Replacement parts and repair kits are usually available from the dealership where the door was purchased or by writing to the manufacturer.

CELLAR DOORS

Many homeowners expand their living space by making the basement more usable with a cellar door. The cellar door (Fig. 3-52) is designed to

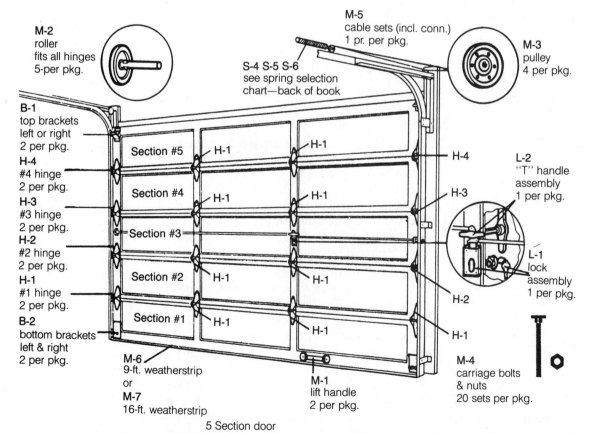

Fig. 3-51. An example of a sectional garage door.

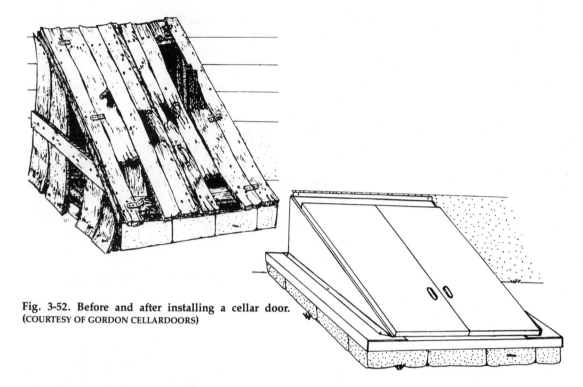

Fig. 3-52. Before and after installing a cellar door.
(COURTESY OF GORDON CELLARDOORS)

offer an outside entrance to the cellar so it can be used for storage, a workshop, a family room, or even bedrooms.

The first step is to decide how you will use your basement and to lay out a plan showing where various activities will take place (Fig. 3-53). Locate the new entrance where it does not interfere with partitions, utilities, piping, or with any construction outside. The door should provide a convenient traffic pattern with relation to the inside basement stairway. It should be located away from any potential hazards, such as the furnace, fireplace, or garage (Fig. 3-54). Locate the entrance where the outside grade is lowest to save steps in and out. Be sure the grade slopes away from the area to provide drainage.

At the chosen location, measure the height of the grade above your basement floor. Add any height required to provide the sloping grade. If you have questions, refer to the Areaway Construction Guide (Fig. 3-55).

Draw vertical lines on the foundation to indicate the location and width of the opening to be made, then stake off the area to be excavated. Allow at least a foot all around for the footing and to apply waterproofing.

Figure 3-56 illustrates how the areaway is turned into your new basement entry. Figure 3-57 shows plans for concrete block courses. Figure 3-58 illustrates how blocks are placed on the footings. Figure 3-59 shows you what the accessway will look like when the blocks are completed

Check Out Receipt

Huntingdon Valley Library
215-947-5138
hvlibrary.org

Monday, July 24, 2017 2:04:11 PM

Title: 1916, the Irish rebellion [videorecording
 (DVD)]
Due: 07/31/2017

Title: Doors, windows, and skylights
Due: 08/14/2017

Title: Windows and doors
Due: 08/14/2017

Total items: 3

Thank You and Come again soon!

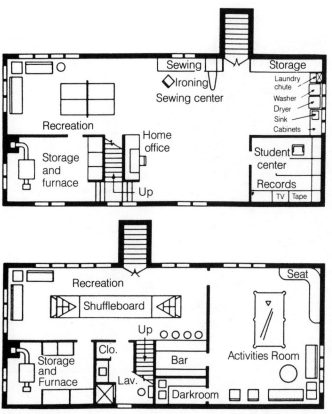

Fig. 3-53. Two floor plans that illustrate the expansion of usable cellar floor space provided by cellar doors.

and before the door, stair stringer, and stair steps are installed. The cellar door should be attached last.

ATTIC DOORS

The simplest attic door is a piece of wood that covers an entrance to the attic and can be lifted out when needed. Installation of an attic door means building a frame—usually of 2 by 4s inserted between rafters—and placing a lip on the inside of the frame to hold the loose door in place.

The folding attic stairway is more complex and functional. It provides both a door and a stairway into upper levels (Fig. 3-60). Using a rough opening of about 2 by 4 or 4¹/₂ feet, the folding stairway can be easily installed in a few hours. The stairway is operated by a handle or cord that is pulled down to lower the door and drop the stairs, which unfold to the floor. These units are available through most larger building materials and hardware stores.

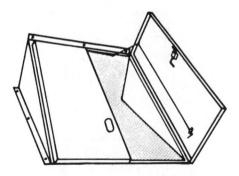

Fig. 3-54. Two types of cellar doors.

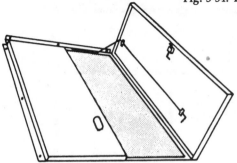

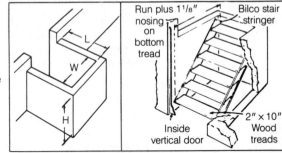

Fig. 3-55. Areaway Construction Guide. (COURTESY OF THE BILCO CO.)

Height of Grade Above Finished Basement Floor Will Be:	Build Areaway To These (Inside) Dimensions:			Use This Bilco Door And Extension		Use These Bilco Stair Stringers & Extensions (Size E Extension Has 3-Tread Run)	Stringer Unit Has 8¼" Rise, 8⅛" Run and ⅛" Nosing	
	H*	L	W	Door Size	Extension Size		Treads in Areaway	Run⁺ in Areaway
2'0" to 2'7"‡	2'9"	3'4"	3'8"	SL	None	(Not Available)	3	2'2¼"
2'8" to 3'3"	3'5¼"	3'4"	3'8"	SL	None	SL	4	2'10⅝"
4'0" to 4'7"‡‡	4'9¾"	4'6"	3'4"	O	None	O	6	4'3⅜"
4'8" to 5'4"‡‡	5'6"	5'0"	3'8"	B	None	B	7	4'11¾"
5'5" to 6'0"	6'2¼"	5'8"	4'0"	C	None	C	8	5'8⅛"
6'1" to 6'8"	6'10½"	6'8"	4'0"	C	12"	O+E	9	6'4½"
6'9" to 7'4"	7'6¾"	7'2"	4'0"	C	18"	B+E	10	7'0⅞"
7'5" to 8'1"	8'3"	7'9"	4'0"	C	24"	C+E	11	7'9¼"

*Above Finished Basement Floor   ‡Maximum House Wall 7'1"   ‡‡Maximum House Wall 7'4"   ⁺Run plus 1⅛" Nosing on Bottom Tread

Fig. 3-56. The areaway and footing for
a cellar door.

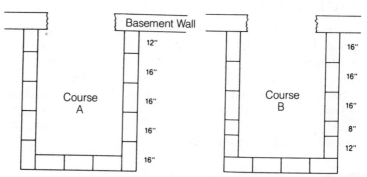

Fig. 3-57. Plans for concrete block courses.

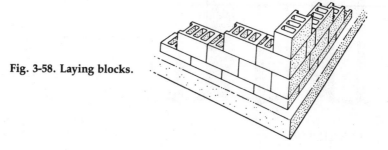

Fig. 3-58. Laying blocks.

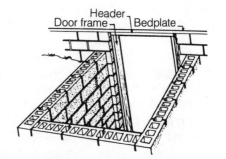

Fig. 3-59. The cellar doorway.

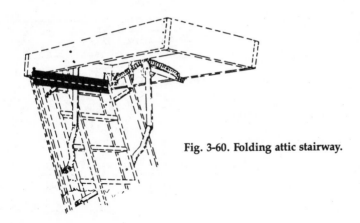

Fig. 3-60. Folding attic stairway.

FOLDING DOORS

There are many folding door systems on the market, but most use the same principles (Fig. 3-61). A track is strung along the ceiling and/or floor to contain rollers attached to narrow hinged panels. When stretched open, these panels become a barrier that closes off entry to a closet, room, or section of a building. Folding doors and partitions are used in homes, offices, schools, churches, and conference centers. Panels are made of wood, vinyl, fiberglass, or metal. Nearly all are available with fire-retardant cores or finishes.

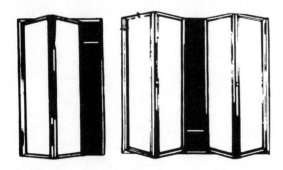

Fig. 3-61. Single and double bifold doors.

SHOWER DOORS

Shower doors and tub enclosures theoretically are designed to keep water off the floor (Fig. 3-62). Figure 3-63 illustrates how shower doors are installed.

First measure the opening at the tub rim and cut the track $3/16$ inch less than the opening. Set the side wall jambs over the track and align all three squarely so that the doors will roll without binding. Mark for the holes in the wall through the holes in the jambs.

Then remove the jambs and track. Drill the holes in the wall with a $3/16$-inch drill bit and insert wall anchors. Run caulk under the track and

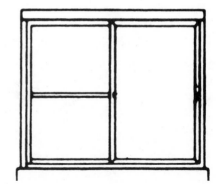

Fig. 3-62. Tub enclosure doors.

set it on the tub rim. Make sure that the drain holes face in toward the tub or shower area. Set the side jambs over the track and secure them with screws through the bumpers.

Cut the header or top track $1/16$ inch less than the opening across the top of the jambs, then slip the header over the jambs.

Attach rollers to the top of the door with screws and attach guides to the bottom of panels by tapping them into place. Lift the door into the header, place the rollers on the track and lower the door into the channel in the bottom track. When adjustments are made, tighten all roller screws completely. Repeat for the second door.

Install the towel bars with screws and mounting brackets if provided. Caulk the entire unit on the inside (directions for caulking are in chapter 7).

MAKING DOOR REPAIRS

As most doors are partially or entirely made of wood, they often crack, split, and warp. In addition, daily use wears out hardware. These situations can often be repaired with common tools and common sense.

To remove a door from its hinges, simply insert a wedge, such as a screwdriver, between the hinge pin head and the hinge itself (Fig. 3-64). Force the head up and out. Always remove the bottom hinge pin first and then move upward. Replace the hinge pins from top to bottom.

A wood plane, called a jack or bench plane, is best for smoothing out door edges. Use a plane with the longest sole you have and a blade wider than the edge of the door. Work from the edge to the center if planning across the grain, and from the center of the rail to the edge if planning with the grain.

A lightly warped door—where the door hits the stop before the latch catches—can be corrected easily by placing a small shim behind the appropriate edge of the hinge.

A heavily warped door may need a 1-by-1 or 1-by-2 support screwed to it to correct the warp. You can bow the support by pouring hot water over it while it lays across a fulcrum. The bowed support can then be cinched down to the door, correcting the door's bow.

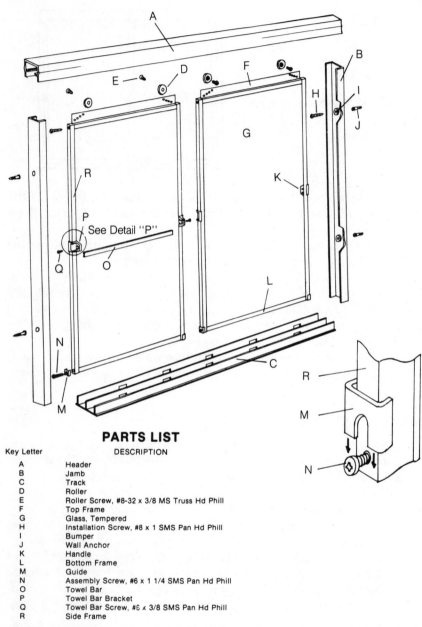

PARTS LIST

Key Letter	DESCRIPTION
A	Header
B	Jamb
C	Track
D	Roller
E	Roller Screw, #8-32 x 3/8 MS Truss Hd Phill
F	Top Frame
G	Glass, Tempered
H	Installation Screw, #8 x 1 SMS Pan Hd Phill
I	Bumper
J	Wall Anchor
K	Handle
L	Bottom Frame
M	Guide
N	Assembly Screw, #6 x 1 1/4 SMS Pan Hd Phill
O	Towel Bar
P	Towel Bar Bracket
Q	Towel Bar Screw, #6 x 3/8 SMS Pan Hd Phill
R	Side Frame

Fig. 3-63. Installation and parts for tub enclosure doors.

Fig. 3-64. Removing door hinge pins.

If the strike plate is too high or low, simply remove it and move the mortise up or down as needed. Replace it and fill in the vacated area with wood putty.

Sliding doors often have adjustment screws on the bottom rollers. Check your unit on the ends and edges to see what adjustments are available. A simple adjustment usually will put it back on track. Check the condition of the rollers. Plastic ones tend to wear down and become unadjustable with age. They may need to be replaced.

4

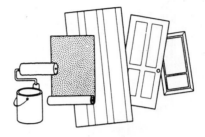

Selecting and Installing Windows

Not too long ago, most homeowners considered windows merely something to gaze through on rainy days. Windows basically were taken for granted. Style was the main consideration. As fuel and utility bills increase, however, homeowners are quickly learning that poorly designed, constructed, and placed windows can cost money.

Windows don't have to be an energy burden. They can be an energy asset and can actually reduce heating and air conditioning costs. How? Windows can bring sunlight into a home during the winter and then prevent its warmth from escaping outdoors. In many instances, the solar heat gain exceeds the windows' heat loss, thereby providing heat during the colder months.

Windows also keep cooled air inside a home during the summer and insulate it from outside heat. In addition, windows can bring cooling breezes into a home when opened during the summer, which can help reduce the air conditioning load. By using daylight as a free source of illumination during all seasons, windows can lower the need for artificial lighting.

TYPES OF WINDOWS

The principle types of windows are double-hung, casement, stationary, awning, and horizontal sliding (Fig. 4-1). They may be made of wood or metal. Heat loss through metal frames and sashes is much greater than through similar wooden units. Glass blocks are sometimes used to admit light in places where transparency or ventilation is not required.

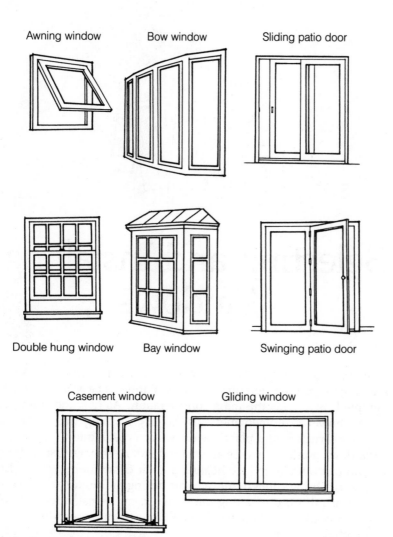

Awning window   Bow window   Sliding patio door

Double hung window   Bay window   Swinging patio door

Casement window   Gliding window

Fig. 4-1. Common window types.

Insulated glass, used both for stationary and movable sashes, consists of two or more sheets of spaced glass with hermetically sealed edges (Fig. 4-2). This type of window is more resistant to heat loss than one with a single thickness of glass and is often used without a storm sash.

Wooden sashes and window frames should be made from a clear grade of all-heartwood stock or decay-resistant wood species or from wood that has been given a preservative treatment. Species commonly used include ponderosa and other pines, cedar, cypress, redwood, and spruce.

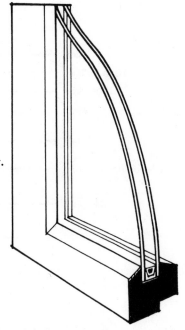

Fig. 4-2. Cross section of the insulated window.

Double-Hung Windows

The double-hung window is perhaps the most familiar window type. It consists of upper and lower sashes that slide vertically in separate grooves in the side jambs or in full-width metal weatherstripping (Fig. 4-3). This type of window provides a maximum face opening for ventilation of one-half the total window area. Each sash is provided with springs, balances, or compression weatherstripping to hold it in place in any location. Compression weatherstripping prevents air infiltration, provides tension, and acts as a counterbalance. Several types allow the sash to be removed for easy painting or repair.

The side and top frame jambs are made of nominal 1-inch lumber (Fig. 4-4), which can be used with a drywall or plaster interior. Sills are made from nominal 2-inch lumber and are sloped at about 3 in 12 for good drainage (Fig. 4-4d). Sashes are normally $1^3/8$ inches thick. Wooden combination storm and screen windows are usually $1^1/8$ inches thick.

The sash may be divided into several lights by small wooden members called muntins (Figs. 4-5 and 4-6). A ranch style house may look best when the top and bottom sashes are divided into two horizontal lights. A cape cod house usually has each sash divided into six or eight lights. This simplifies painting and other maintenance.

Assembled frames are placed in the rough opening over strips of building paper, which is put around the perimeter to minimize air infiltration. The frame is plumbed and nailed to the side studs and header

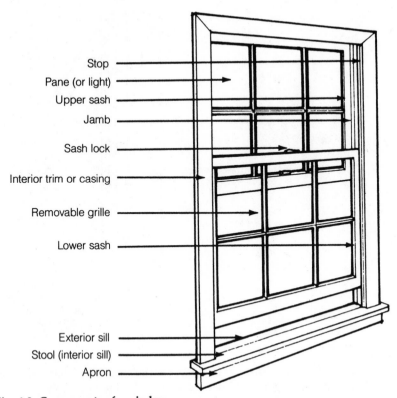

Stop
Pane (or light)
Upper sash
Jamb
Sash lock
Interior trim or casing
Removable grille
Lower sash
Exterior sill
Stool (interior sill)
Apron

Fig. 4-3. Components of a window.

through the casings or the blind stops at the sides. Where nails are exposed, such as on the casing, use the corrosion-resistant type.

Hardware for double-hung windows includes the sash lifts, which are fastened to the bottom rail, and sash locks or fasteners, which are located at the meeting rail. Sash locks not only lock the window, but draw the sash together to provide a tight fit. Sash lifts may be eliminated by providing a finger groove in the bottom rail.

Double-hung windows can be arranged as a single unit, a double or mullion unit, or in groups of three or more. One or two double-hung windows on each side of a large stationary, insulated window are often used to effect a window wall. Such large openings must be framed with headers large enough to carry roof loads.

Casement Windows

Casement windows consist of a side-hinged sash, which is usually designed to swing outward (Fig. 4-7). This type can be made more weather tight than the in-swinging style. Winter protection is obtained

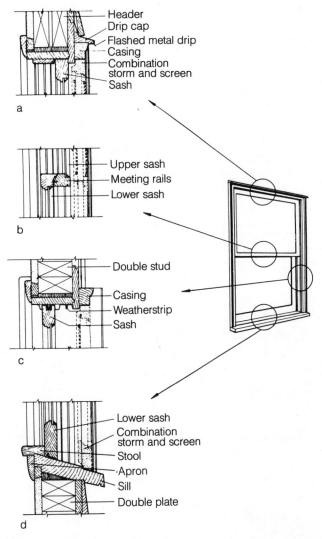

Fig. 4-4. Double-hung windows: (a) head jamb, (b) meeting rails, (c) side jambs, and (d) sill.

with a storm sash or by using insulated glass in the sash. Screens are located inside these out-swinging windows. One advantage to the casement window over the double-hung type is that the entire window area can be opened for ventilation.

Weatherstripping is also provided for this type of window. Units are usually received from the factory entirely assembled with hardware in place. Closing hardware consists of a rotary operator and sash lock. As in the double-hung units, casement sashes can be used as a pair or in com-

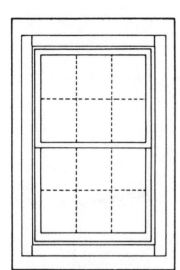

Fig. 4-5. Double-hung sashes can be divided into several lights by small wood members called muntins.

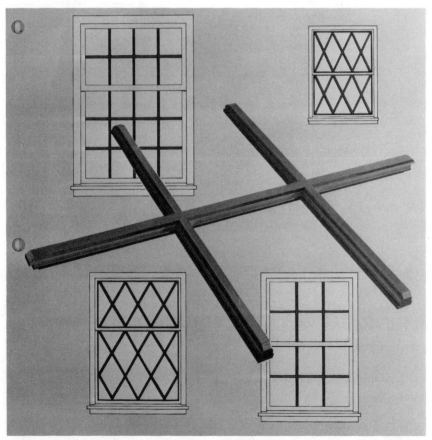

Fig. 4-6. Artificial muntins can be made with removable wood grilles. (COURTESY OF WEBB MANUFACTURING INC.)

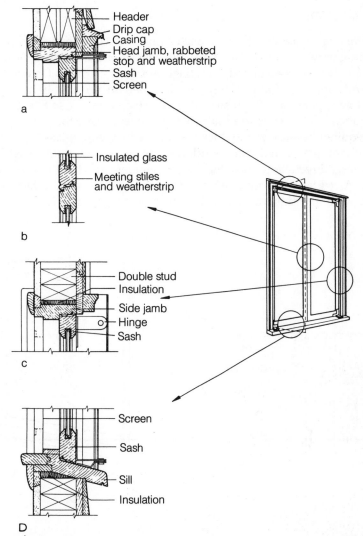

Fig. 4-. .ᵈ Out-swinging casement sash: (a) head jamb, (b) meeting stiles, (c) side jambs, and (d) sill.

binations of two or more pairs. Style variations are achieved by divided lights. Snap-in muntins provide a small, multiple-pane appearance for traditional styling.

Metal sashes are sometimes used. Because of low insulating value, they should be installed carefully to prevent condensation and frosting on the interior surfaces during cold weather. A full storm-window unit is sometimes necessary to eliminate this problem in cold climates.

Stationary Windows

Stationary windows that are used alone or in combination with double-hung or casement windows usually consist of a wooden sash with a large single light of insulated glass (Figs. 4-8 and 4-9) that is fastened permanently into the frame. They are designed to provide light and an attractive appearance. Because of their size (sometimes 6 to 8 feet wide), a 1³/₄-inch thick sash is used to provide strength. This thickness is usually required because of the thickness of the insulating glass.

Other types of stationary windows may be used without a sash. The glass is set directly into rabbeted frame members and held in place with stops. As with all window sash units, puttying the back and face of the glass, with or without a stop, will assure moisture resistance.

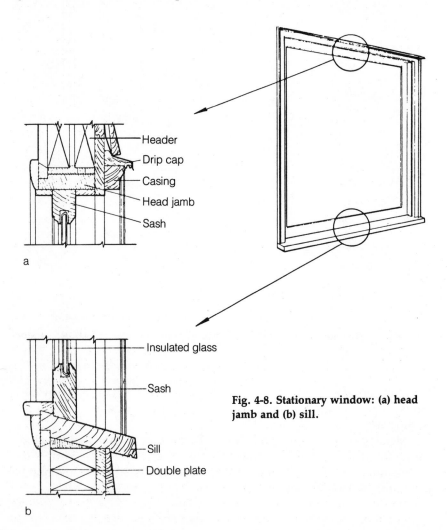

a

Header
Drip cap
Casing
Head jamb
Sash

Insulated glass

Sash

Sill

Double plate

b

Fig. 4-8. Stationary window: (a) head jamb and (b) sill.

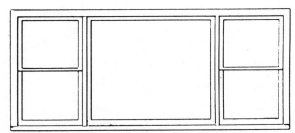

Fig. 4-9. Stationary windows can be used in combination with other types.

Awning Windows

An awning window unit consists of a frame in which one or more operative sashes are installed (Fig. 4-10). They often are made up for a large window wall and consist of three or more units in width and height.

A sash of the awning type is made to swing outward at the bottom. A similar unit, called the hopper type, is one in which the top of the sash swings inward. Both types provide protection from rain when open.

Jambs for these windows are usually $1^{1}/_{16}$ inches or more thick because they are rabbeted, while the sill is at least $1^{5}/_{16}$ inches thick when two or more sashes are used in a complete frame. Each sash may also be provided with an individual frame, so that any combination in width and height can be used. Awning or hopper window units may consist of a combination of one or more fixed sashes with the remainder being the operable type. Operable sashes are provided with hinges, pivots, and sash supporting arms.

Weatherstripping, storm sashes, and screens are usually provided. The storm sash is eliminated when the windows are glazed with insulating glass.

Horizontal Sliding Windows

Horizontal sliding windows appear similar to casement sashes. The sashes slide horizontally in separate tracks or guides, which are located on the sill and head jamb. Multiple window openings consist of two or more single units and may be used when a window-wall effect is desired. Weatherstripping, water-repellent preservative treatments, and sometimes hardware are included in the factory-assembled units.

Miscellaneous Windows

Other windows that are installed in homes and offices are designed to enhance views, ventilation, light entrance, function, or decoration (Fig. 4-11). The greenhouse window is built to be both functional and decorative, and offer light, ventilation, and a sunny place to grow plants. Greenhouse windows come in various sizes and designs and can be

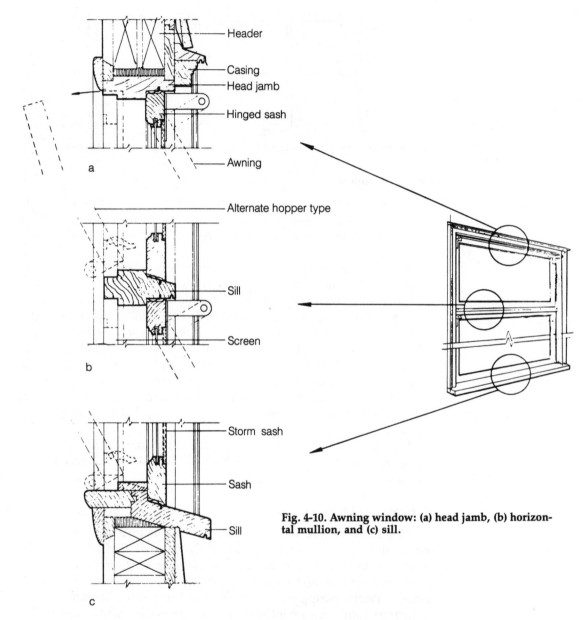

Header

Casing
Head jamb

Hinged sash

Awning

a

Alternate hopper type

Sill

Screen

b

Storm sash

Sash

Sill

c

Fig. 4-10. Awning window: (a) head jamb, (b) horizontal mullion, and (c) sill.

installed in most standard window openings. Installation is similar to other windows, except that careful consideration must be given to the weight and support of the window so that plants in the unit don't over-burden the frame and cause it to sag or fall out. Units come with specific installation instructions.

Patio doors are both doors and windows (Fig. 4-12). They are similar to horizontal sliding windows, only larger.

Fig. 4-11. Half-round decorative window. (COURTESY OF WEBB MANUFACTURING INC.)

Bay windows give a home an old-fashioned look, as well as provide light and a view. Some offer window seats, while others are open to the floor. Bay windows come in standardized sizes from 6 to 12 feet wide and from 3¹/₂ to 7 feet high.

Bow windows are similar to bay windows (Fig. 4-13). The difference is that bow units are more graceful, with gently curving glass panes rather than the sharp angles of the bay. Sashes are usually more narrow, and bow windows are often larger than bays. Bow windows come in sizes from 6 to 15 feet wide and 3 to 7 feet high. Both bays and bows can be custom-built by craftsmen or ambitious do-it-yourselfers.

Jalousies are a variation of the awning window and have numerous short, wide panes that are mounted on movable clips and frames (Fig. 4-14). Cranking the operable sash will open all of the glass units at once. They are installed just like awning windows.

Fig. 4-12. The patio door is both a door and a window. (COURTESY OF LOUISIANA PACIFIC CORP.)

BATHROOM WINDOWS

Bathroom windows often create a problem. You want to let in the natural light without allowing any visibility from outside. Many frosted windows and special bathroom windows are available for just such uses. But if you have a clear-pane window in your bathroom, you might not wish to change the entire window. You can still create the effect you need by installing an opaque glass pane.

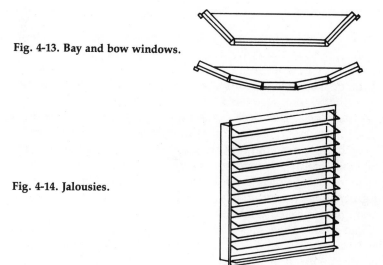

Fig. 4-13. Bay and bow windows.

Fig. 4-14. Jalousies.

Or, you may wish to cover the window. Shutters may fit in with the decor of your home and cover your window nicely. The wood accent can add a touch of elegance. If the window is near the shower, the shutters should be protected from the spray. If the window is over the tub or tub/ shower combination, the window can be inexpensively covered with a second shower curtain, either matching or complementing the first.

Curtains, blinds, and shades are more traditional window coverings that can be used in the bathroom. All allow you the choice of letting in all or part, of the natural light.

SIZING WINDOWS

Windows come in just about every size imaginable. Each manufacturer sizes windows just a bit differently, so you should be aware of how each is measured before you purchase the unit.

Generally, the size of the window is noted by the actual size of the opening or sash. Standard sash opening widths for double- and single-hung windows are measured in 4-inch increments with widths from 20 to 40 inches and heights from 34 to 62 inches. You can buy a window that measures 28 by 46 or 36 by 54.

Casement windows come in fewer size variations and there is a variety of sash groupings: two, three, four, or five.

Awning windows offer style and size variety. Widths range from 18 to 52 inches and heights from 38 to 72 inches. There are smaller sizes for single-unit awning windows.

Horizontal sliding windows and patio doors come in widths of 36, 48, 60, and 72 inches and heights of 24, 34, 48, 56, and 60 inches. Patio doors are typically 80 inches high.

BUYING GLASS

Whether you're buying a new window or a piece of replacement glass, you should understand what glass is and how it is measured and graded. Most manufactured glass is soda-lime glass, an alkali silicate glass made insoluble by adding a small amount of calcium oxide. Lead glass or flint glass is also used.

Window glass is typically called sheet glass and is formed in vertical sheets. Sheet glass typically comes in thicknesses ranging from $3/32$ inch to $1/8$ inch. Single strength is thin glass that weighs about 19 ounces per square foot. Double-strength glass is $1/8$ inch thick and weighs 26 ounces per square foot. Typical grades of glass are A (superior), B (standard), and greenhouse (lower quality). AA grade is available by special order. Thicker glass is called crystal sheet.

Plate glass is sheet glass that has been ground and polished on both sides to a uniform thickness, with little or no distortion. Regular polished plate is used in home construction and is usually $1/4$ inch thick. Larger windows use heavy polished plate glass, which is $3/8$ inch thick or more.

Tempered glass is made by controlled heating and cooling processes that multiply the strength and impact resistance of the glass. Heat-strengthened glass is partially tempered, but it is not a safety glass.

Tinted glass is created by the addition of green-gray or bronze coloring agents to the molten glass, which reduce the impact of the Sun's rays on the final product.

To cope with some of the problems presented by glass as a construction material, glass manufacturers have devised a variety of special window glasses. Because sheet glass is a very poor insulator, large areas of glass permit great heat loss. Glass walls should always be double-glazed, with the two layers of glass locking in an insulating layer of air. Double glazing also eliminates moisture condensation, which can occur when cold air strikes warm glass. However, you must be careful to install the glass properly. Many manufacturers now offer thermal insulating glass that is sealed on the edges and has an air space between two sheets of special plate glass. It is available in standard window sizes.

Tinted glass, either green- or bronze-colored, is often used in modern commercial buildings to inhibit heat absorption, which places a great burden on air-conditioning equipment. The material is expensive, however, and the color distortion, though slight, makes it generally unappealing in residential buildings.

Where safety is important, tempered glass is used. The molten sheets are subject to special cooling processes that increase the material's resistance to breakage. For areas particularly threatened by breakage, wire glass—panels in which a layer of wire mesh is embedded—is available. Its appearance is unattractive, however, and its application is generally limited to inconspicuous areas.

FRAMING WINDOWS IN NEW WALLS

The first step in installing a window in a new wall is to lay out the opening between regular studs (Fig. 4-15). It may be necessary to move an existing stud or to add a new one. Make sure that the distance between the regular studs equals the suggested rough opening width of the window or patio door unit, plus the thickness of two regular wall studs.

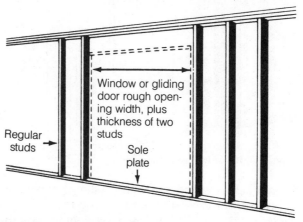

Fig. 4-15. Making the window opening in a wall.

Cut two pieces of header material—2 by 8s, 2 by 10s, or 2 by 12s—equal to the rough opening width of the window unit, plus the thickness of two regular studs. Nail the two pieces of header material together so that the header is as thick as a regular stud.

In most home construction, the header should be 6 feet 10¹/₂ inches from the subfloor (Fig. 4-16). Position the header at this height between the regular studs. Nail through the regular studs into each end of the header to hold it in place until the next step is completed.

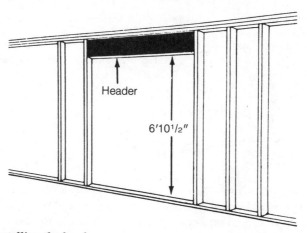

Fig. 4-16. Installing the header.

Cut the jack studs (Fig. 4-17) so that they fit snugly between the sole plate and the header. Nail the jack studs to the regular studs and toenail the jack studs to the header.

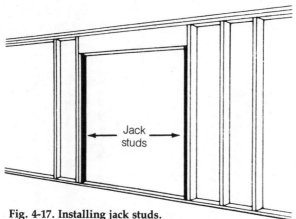

Fig. 4-17. Installing jack studs.

No other framing is needed if you're installing a patio door. If you're installing a window, the next step is to cut the rough sill and cripples from 2 by 4s (Fig. 4-18) so that the opening conforms with the rough opening size of your window. The rough sill length should equal the window unit rough opening width. The distance between the top of the rough sill and the header should equal the window unit rough opening height. Nail the side cripples to the jack studs. Center and nail the remaining cripples to the rough sill. Place the rough sill on side cripples and nail. Toenail the center cripples to the sole plate.

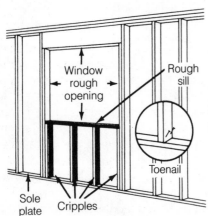

Fig. 4-18. Installing the cripples and rough sill.

In new construction, the next step is to apply exterior sheathing—fiberboard, plywood, foam board, etc.—flush with the rough sill, header, and jack stud framing members (Figs. 4-19 and 4-20). You now are ready to install the window.

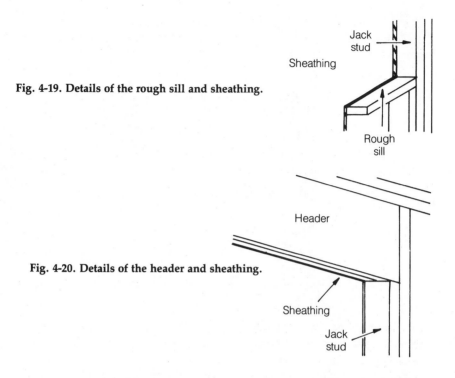

Fig. 4-19. Details of the rough sill and sheathing.

Fig. 4-20. Details of the header and sheathing.

PREPARING EXISTING WALLS

If you are replacing a window in your home or building, the steps are a little different. The first step, logically, is to remove the old window.

Steel casement windows are usually secured by screws to a wooden frame around the window opening. To remove, first locate the screws. They can often be found under the sash itself on venting or operating units. Open the sash and look at the frame for screws. Around picture window units they may be on the outside of the frame just in front of the glass and covered with putty. After the screws have been located and any putty cleared away, the screws can be removed. It may be necessary to use a cold chisel to cut inaccessible or tight screws, or they may be drilled out. Take care to prevent injury from breaking glass. Run nylon filament tape over all glass surfaces before attempting to remove the window from its opening.

Aluminum double-hung or sliding windows are usually secured by screws through the exterior flange or through the jamb itself (Fig. 4-21). When screwed through the jamb, screws are often found in the sash run and are attached to the wooden wall framing. Remove all the screws holding the frame to the wall members. Again, use a cold chisel to cut inaccessible or tight screws, or drill them out. Sometimes the frame is attached to wall studs with the flange beneath the exterior siding. Most aluminum frames may be pulled out of the opening. If necessary, use a

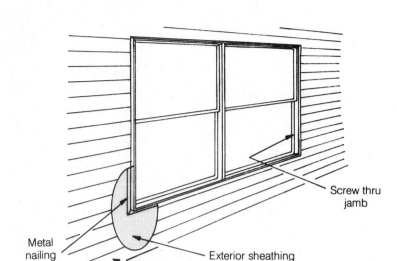

Fig. 4-21. Securing aluminum double-hung or sliding windows by screws through the exterior flange or the jamb.

saber saw with the proper blade to cut the flange between the frame and the wall stud. The unit can be removed from the opening after glass is taped as previously described.

Wooden windows are usually more difficult to remove. Begin by removing the inside stops of the window with a small pry bar. Use a utility knife to break the paint bind between the stops and the wall or trim. Remove all interior trim. If it will be reused, use a pry bar to gently pull off all members at once, as most trim is nailed together at the miter joint. Remove nails by pulling them through the wood with a pair of nippers. If there is a metal sash run, remove it by pulling the nails with a small pry bar.

The lower sash should also be removed. Carefully cut any weight ropes or cords, or simply remove them if possible. Pull out the sash carefully to avoid breaking the glass. To remove the upper sash, all parting stop members and the metal sash runs must first be removed with a small pry bar. Remove the upper sash by pulling out one side at a time. To remove the window frame from the opening, saw it completely through the sill. With this removed, the entire frame can be pried out and easily collapsed.

When the old window is out, you can modify the wall to the appropriate rough opening size by following the instructions offered previously for framing windows in new walls (Figs. 4-22 through 4-26).

INSTALLING WINDOWS

When the rough opening has been framed and found to be plumb and level, the window unit can be inserted into the opening and allowed to

Fig. 4-22. Replacing an old window. Step 1: carefully remove the old casing. (COUR-TESY OF MARVIN WINDOWS)

rest on the rough sill so that a proper fit is ensured. To prevent operating and weathertightness problems later, check to make sure the window unit is plumb and level before fastening it to the opening. Check the window to make sure it is level across the sill and head. Check for plumb two ways: side-to-side and front-to-back. To check for side-to-side plumb, use a carpenter's square at the corners of the unit or a level at the side of the frame. To check for front-to-back plumb, place the level on the outside face of the frame to make sure the window is not tilted outward or inward.

To correct errors in plumb or level, use a pry bar to raise the sill of the window. When it is in position, drive a nail through the head flange and into the rough framing member. If the sill is raised, be sure to shim the

Fig. 4-23. Step 2: measure the rough opening between the 2 by 4 window framing. (COURTESY OF MARVIN WINDOWS)

sides to keep the jamb in a straight, plumb position. Check again for plumb and level, and nail the opposite corner of the window into the frame. Finally, check again for plumb and level, then completely nail in the window. Metal window sashes are usually installed with screws rather than nails. Follow the instructions packed with each window unit (Figs. 4-27 through 4-38).

INSTALLING GLASS-BLOCK PANELS

Glass-block panels are simple to install and offer both decorative beauty and practical light transmission. Glass-block windows can even be installed with operable glass sections for ventilation (Fig. 4-39).

Here are simple instructions for installing preassembled glass-block panels in wood and masonry walls. Before ordering a glass-block panel, carefully measure the opening from the outside of the house. Measure the width of the opening from the wooden jamb or from the aluminum covering the wood or brick opening. Measure the height of the opening from the top of the windowsill to the header (Fig. 4-40).

Fig. 4-24. Step 3: measure the exterior size of the window. (COUR-TESY OF MARVIN WINDOWS)

Remove the movable section of the window. From the outside of the house, pry the bottom frame away from the sill using a crowbar. Cut the frame where necessary and remove the frame all the way around the opening (Fig. 4-41).

It may be necessary to adjust the window opening to the proper size by cutting the opening if it is too small or by adding 1 by 4 or 2 by 4 lumber if the opening is too large. Fasten a wooden or metal stop around the inside of the frame, place the glass-block panel into the opening, and shim where necessary (Fig. 4-42). Fasten the stop around the outside of the window frame and caulk it to ensure tightness (Figs. 4-43 through 4-45).

Fig. 4-25. Step 4: once the new window arrives, remove the old window from the outside. (COURTESY OF MARVIN WINDOWS)

INSTALLING PATIO DOORS

The first step in installing a new or replacement patio door is to make sure that the rough opening is the correct size for the unit. This is done by measuring and then by placing the unit within the frame. Check the rough opening for plumb, level, and square. If the opening is too wide or high, fill it with boards of the appropriate thickness to bring the opening to the specified rough opening dimensions. Caulk beneath the boards before installation.

Run caulking compound across the underside of the sill to provide a tight seal between the door sill and the floor. If the door frame is unassembled, follow the included assembly instructions. If the sill is placed on concrete, use sill filler insulation beneath.

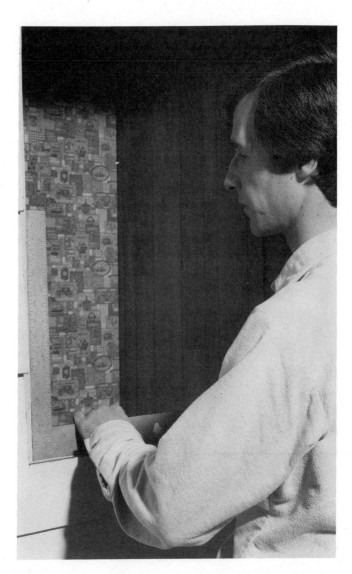

Fig. 4-26. Step 5: check the rough opening to make sure it's square. (COURTESY OF MAR-VIN WINDOWS)

Position the frame in the opening from the outside. Apply pressure to the sill to properly distribute caulking compound. Temporarily secure the frame in the opening by using clamps to draw the flanges tight against the sheathing. Check jambs for plumb, and the sill and head for level. Shim between the jambs and rough opening members. Complete the frame installation. Apply loosely packed insulation in all spaces between the frame and the rough opening.

Position the stationary door panel in the outer run. Force the door into the rabbet of the side jamb with a 2 by 4 wedge. The panel is in the correct position when the edge lines up with the scribe line on the sill

Fig. 4-27. Step 6: insert and center the new window in the opening from the outside. (COURTESY OF MARVIN WINDOWS)

and predrilled holes for brackets at the head jamb, or other manufacturer's markings. Secure the stationary panel to the frame by screwing through the stationary sill filler. Secure the head with the bracket applied to the top rail. Then screw through the parting stop.

The operating panel should then be placed on the sill track. Tip the door in at the top and slide it to the closed position. Position and secure the head stop with screws. Check the door's operation. If the door sticks, binds, or is not square in the frame, locate the two adjustment sockets on the inside bottom rail of the panel. Unscrew the caps, insert a screwdriver, and turn the screws to raise or lower the door. Replace the caps. Finally, install the latch and threshold (Fig. 4-46).

Fig. 4-28. Step 7: partially nail the window into the lower corner of the casing. (COUR-TESY OF MARVIN WINDOWS)

INSTALLING WINDOW TRIM

The casing around the window frames on the interior of the house should be the same pattern as that used around the interior door frames (chapter 3). Other trim that is used for a double-hung window frame includes the sash stops, stool, and apron (Fig. 4-47). Another type of trim encloses the entire opening with casing (Fig. 4-48). The stool is then a filler member between the bottom sash rail and the bottom casing.

The stool is the horizontal trim member that laps the windowsill and extends beyond the casing at the sides, with each end notched against the plastered wall. The apron serves as a finish member below the stool. The window stool is the first piece of window trim to be installed. It is notched and fitted against the edge of the jamb and the plaster line, with the outside edge being flush against the bottom rail of the window sash (Fig. 4-47). The stool is blind-nailed at the ends so that the casing and the stop will cover the nailheads. Predrilling is usually necessary to prevent splitting. The stool should also be nailed at the midpoint of the sill and to the apron with finishing nails. Face nailing to the sill is sometimes substi-tuted or supplemented with toenailing of the outer edge to the sill.

Fig. 4-29. Step 8: level the sill. (COURTESY OF MARVIN WINDOWS)

The casing is applied and nailed as described for door frames, except that the inner edge is flush with the inner face of the jambs so that the stop will cover the joint between the jamb and casing. The window stops are then nailed to the jambs so that the window sash slides smoothly. Channel-type weatherstripping often includes full-width metal sub-jambs into which the upper and lower sashes slide, replacing the parting strip. Stops are located against these instead of the sash to provide a small amount of pressure. The apron is cut to a length equal to the outer width of the casing line. It is nailed to the windowsill and to the 2-by-4-inch framing sill below.

When the casing is used to finish the bottom of the window frame as well as the sides and top, the narrow stool butts against the side window jamb. Casing is then mitered at the bottom corners and nailed as previously described.

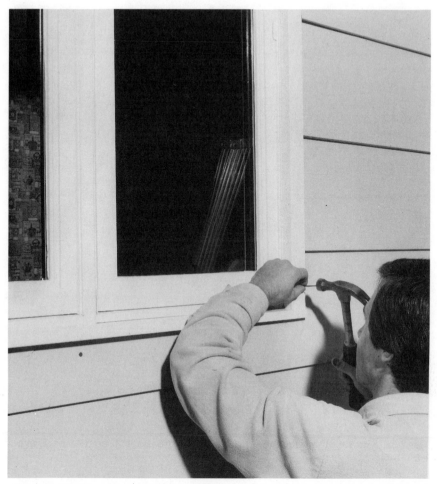

Fig. 4-30. Step 9: with the sill level, finish nailing the bottom corner. (COURTESY OF MARVIN WINDOWS)

REPLACING WINDOW GLASS

The most common repair necessary for windows is replacing broken window glass. Although removing and replacing window panes is not a difficult job, it does require attention and skill. Wear work gloves to protect your hands while taking broken glass from the frame. If shattered, glass sections can usually be lifted out easily and safely. Remove the top pieces first to make sure they don't fall on your hands. If the glass is only cracked, you may want to remove the putty around the glass first before taking the glass out. If in doubt, break up the glass with a hard object and remove it carefully.

Fig. 4-31. Step 10: plumb the lower half of one of the jambs. (COURTESY OF MARVIN WINDOWS)

Old putty can be removed from the window frame with a wood chisel, a putty knife, or a pocketknife. Take time to remove every trace of old putty and debris. Be sure to remove the glazier's points as you remove the putty. Glazier's points are small metal triangles driven into the frame underneath the putty to hold the glass in place (Fig. 4-49). Old, stubborn putty can be removed by running an electric soldering iron just ahead of your putty knife to heat and soften the putty.

If you are replacing glass in an old wooden window, apply linseed oil to the wood around the frame and allow it to soak into the wood. The linseed oil will extend the life of both the wood and the new putty.

With the old putty and glass removed from the frame, you can insert the replacement glass. Be sure you are installing a replacement glass of the correct size. The new pane should be just a fraction of an inch smaller than the window area it is to fill. If it isn't, cut it to the proper size with a good glass cutter. Snap off the excess with a pair of pliers.

Fig. 4-32. Step 11: nail through the casing halfway up. (COURTESY OF MARVIN WINDOWS)

Insert the new window pane firmly into the frame and move it around as needed to seat it in the putty. Hold the pane in position with one hand and insert a glazier's point on each side to keep it firmly in place. Glazier's points should then be installed about 4 inches apart around the perimeter of the pane. Lay each point flat against the glass and start it into the wood with the point of your chisel.

The putty should be applied next. Because new putty is extremely difficult to paint, you may want to purchase colored putty or mix your own by blending appropriate paint with the putty. Make a test batch before coloring all the putty you need. Knead and work the putty on an old piece of glass. Roll the putty into pencil-size rolls or strips. Use your hands to apply the putty strips along the edge of the pane and frame beginning at one corner and going completely around the new piece of glass. Smooth out the putty bead with a clean putty knife (Fig. 4-50). Use a long, even stroke. Take your time. A couple extra minutes will make your glass installation look like a professional job.

Fig. 4-33. Step 12: plumb the upper half of the jamb and nail the top corner. Finally, plumb and nail the other jamb and across the top. (COURTESY OF MARVIN WINDOWS)

Finishing touches are done with a razor blade and common paint. Use the razor blade to touch up the putty after it has dried slightly. When it's dry, you can touch it up with sandpaper. If you plan to paint the putty and frame, wait a couple days until it is completely dry. The drying process will take longer in humid climates and during wet seasons. Use a metal shield or masking tape to ensure that the paint doesn't run over onto the glass.

Sometimes wooden strips or plastic gaskets are used instead of putty to hold window glass in place. Wooden strips can be pried out. Watch for brad nails that hold wooden strips in place. Leftover putty can be re-sealed in an airtight container for later use.

Fig. 4-34. Step 13: inside, block the center of the sill. (COURTESY OF MARVIN WINDOWS)

SOLVING CONDENSATION PROBLEMS

Condensation can be a problem in both old and new homes—a problem that can cause both seen and unseen damage to windows, doors, walls, paint, and structural wood.

A small amount of fog in the lower corners of your windows now and then shouldn't bother you. Condensation that blocks whole windows with fog or frost and water that runs off windows to stain woodwork or wall coverings should bother you. The visible damage is bad enough, but the unseen damage—exterior paint blisters, moist insulation and plasterboard—can be both costly and unsafe.

Condensation, humidity, water vapor, moisture, and steam are vaporous water. A high level of water vapor in the air is called high humidity. Wet air is subject to vapor pressure; it tries to flow toward drier

Fig. 4-35. Step 14: shim the jambs top, center, and bottom. (COURTESY OF MARVIN WINDOWS)

air and mix with it. If drier air is outside the window, the moisture collects on the window and forms condensation. It can also pass through walls that don't have built-in vapor barriers.

How much water can be found in your home's air? Studies indicate that cooking for the typical family adds nearly 5 pounds of moisture to a home's air. The weekly laundry typically adds as much as 30 pounds. A shower adds $1/2$ pound, and humans add about 7 pounds per day. A family of four can easily release 150 pounds—more than 18 gallons—of water into their home's air per week.

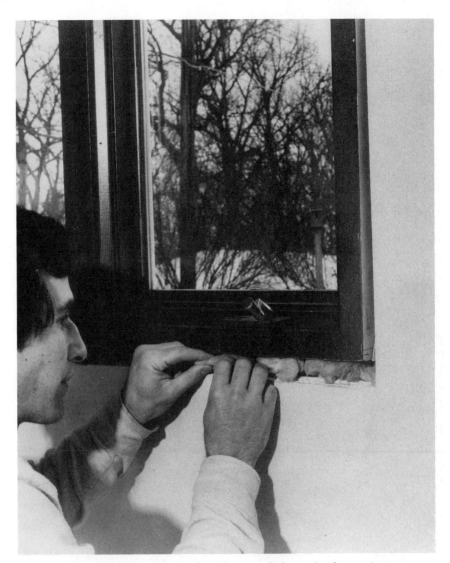

Fig. 4-36. Step 15: add insulation loosely around the entire frame. (COURTESY OF MARVIN WINDOWS)

There are many ways to reduce the humidity in your home. Vapor barriers stop moisture from leaving through walls. Built-in attic vents allow moisture to move into and out of the home. If condensation is forming on your home's windows, here's how to remedy the problem:

- Install double-glazing or double-insulating glass, or install storm windows.

- Shut off the furnace humidifier and any other humidifying devices in your home during times of dry humidity outside.

Fig. 4-37. Step 16: apply inside casing. (COURTESY OF MARVIN WINDOWS)

- Be sure that vents and louvers in the attic or basement crawl spaces are open and that they are large enough for your home.

- Run kitchen or other ventilating fans longer than normal to clear out saturated air.

- Open the fireplace damper to allow moisture to escape easily.

Fig. 4-38. Step 17: caulk around the outside of the unit to fill the crack between the siding and the new window. (COURTESY OF MARVIN WINDOWS)

- If possible, air out your house a few minutes each day. Air out the kitchen, laundry, and bathrooms during or just following use.

- If troublesome condensation persists, consider installing an outside air intake for your furnace, additional venting for gas-burning heaters and appliances, and more ventilating fans.

Condensation is a symptom of too much humidity in your home. Humidity can be checked with an instrument called a psychrometer and should be no more than 40 to 60% for comfort. High humidity can damage walls, wood, and even affect human health over a long period. Proper windows and other solutions can reduce condensation and lower the humidity level in your home, making it a more enjoyable place to live.

Fig. 4-39. Remember to install insulation around the patio door frame before placing the casing.

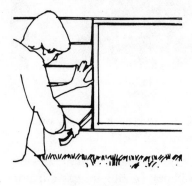

Fig. 4-40. Measuring the opening for glass-block panel installation.

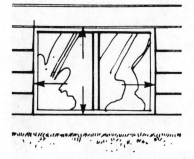

Fig. 4-41. Remove the frame from around the old window.

Fig. 4-42. Place the glass-block panel into the opening and shim where necessary.

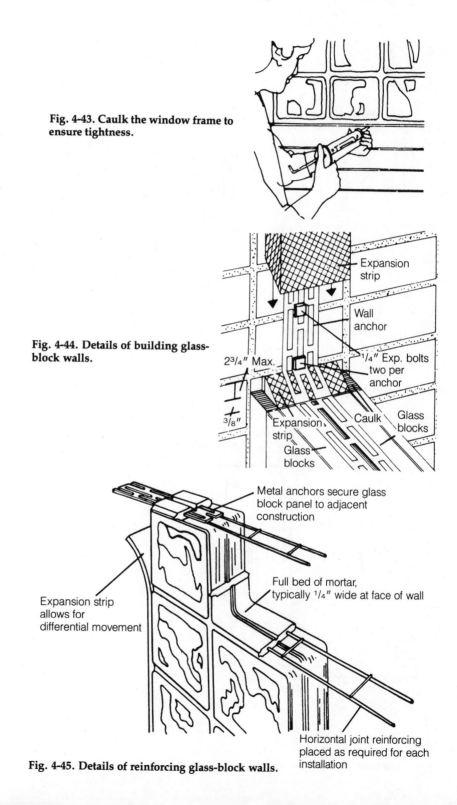

Fig. 4-43. Caulk the window frame to ensure tightness.

Fig. 4-44. Details of building glass-block walls.

Expansion strip

Wall anchor

$2^3/_4''$ Max.

$1/_4''$ Exp. bolts two per anchor

$3/_8''$

Expansion strip

Caulk

Glass blocks

Glass blocks

Metal anchors secure glass block panel to adjacent construction

Full bed of mortar, typically $1/_4''$ wide at face of wall

Expansion strip allows for differential movement

Horizontal joint reinforcing placed as required for each installation

Fig. 4-45. Details of reinforcing glass-block walls.

Fig. 4-46. Steps for installing a patio door.

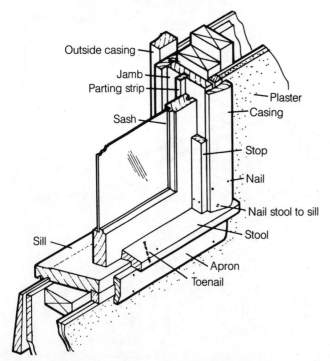

Outside casing

Jamb

Parting strip

Sash

Plaster

Casing

Stop

Nail

Nail stool to sill

Stool

Sill

Apron

Toenail

Fig. 4-47. Installing window trim with stool and apron.

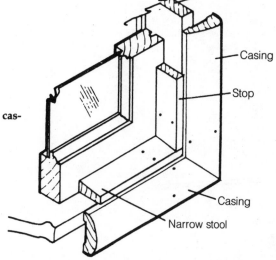

Fig. 4-48. **Installing window trim enclosed with casing.**

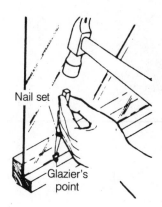

Fig. 4-49. **Setting glazier's points to hold glass in place.**

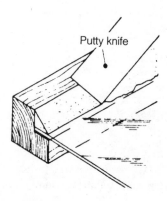

Fig. 4-50. **The putty knife smooths the glazier's putty as it is applied.**

5

Selecting and Installing Skylights

A SKYLIGHT IS AN OPENING IN A ROOF OR CEILING DESIGNED TO ALLOW THE entry of light, a view, or, in some cases, ventilation into an enclosed area. The concept of including ceiling windows in structures is old, but it has become extremely popular in the last two decades with the renewed interest in solar technology. The high cost of heating and lighting also has made skylights more attractive.

ADVANTAGES OF SKYLIGHTS

Skylights offer the only means of introducing daylight into interior rooms that in the past were dark and unattractive. Such rooms include interior bedrooms, bathrooms, utility rooms, and hallways. Another advantage to skylights is that they bring outdoor light indoors without reducing privacy. An entryway or the main living room can be completely illuminated by natural light during the day without losing desired privacy. The natural light tends to lift spirits and makes rooms cheerier than artificial lighting.

Skylights set at the proper angle provide light equally to all parts of a room, not like windows that offer intense light nearby and less light at a distance. Skylights can also be installed where normal vertical windows can not.

DAWN'S EARLY LIGHT

Since man first began constructing buildings, skylights and windows have been used to let in free natural daylight. The first skylights were merely holes in the wall or roof. Now there are attractive modern designs that incorporate the latest materials.

Skylights are considered by architects and designers to be a major component of aesthetically pleasing indoor environments. Many award-winning industrial, commercial, and residential designs include skylights for dramatic and pleasing effects.

Aesthetics are only part of the story, however. Lighting experts know that task visibility improves as illumination increases and that the human eye can easily accommodate the changes in levels of daylight. Typical levels of sunlight in a given locality can be translated to skylight designs, which can provide daylight that meets and often exceeds minimal recommended task lighting levels. Skylights provide savings on installation costs and electricity for electrical lighting systems.

SKYLIGHTS AND ENERGY

Despite the psychological and aesthetic advantages of skylights, the abundance of inexpensive energy in the recent past often prompted homebuilders to meet lighting needs with electrical lighting alone. Windowless schools and commercial buildings were built to cloister the occupants away from the vagaries of daylight.

In Europe, where energy costs have always been high, the per capita use of skylights is about 10 times that of this country. Americans are beginning to realize that skylights actually offer an energy advantage. The conservation and use of solar energy in modern construction and remodeling are demanding a more sophisticated analysis of building energy use. The simple consideration of conductive heat loss or gain is no longer adequate. Also, 100% reliance on mechanical, fossil-fuel consuming systems for heating and cooling—or even for lighting—is proving quite costly. Homebuilders and remodelers are actively seeking methods of supplementing mechanical and electrical systems with natural energy sources directly available from the external environment. Skylights are proving to be one of the most effective methods available—one which doesn't sacrifice aesthetically pleasing living and working space.

SKYLIGHTS IN WINTER

Skylights make direct use of the Sun's light. They transmit solar light to reduce the electrical demand for lighting and efficiently utilize the Sun's heat by functioning as passive solar collectors. Combined with modern skylight fabrication techniques that reduce heat loss, the solar lighting and heating benefits offset heat conduction.

The ability of skylights to offset electrical lighting carries an additional conservation benefit beyond the direct savings of electricity. Electrical lights also produce heat. This heat tends to supplement the output of the building's heating system. The heat produced by electrical lights requires, in effect, two to three times more fossil fuel than the same amount of heat produced directly from the same fuels in the building's heating plant. This is due to the inherent efficiency levels of electricity production and delivery from the power plant to the building. Offsetting some of the electrical lighting through use of skylights not only acts to lower net building energy use, but also helps reduce the nation's consumption of limited supplies of fossil fuels.

In winter, skylights contribute to energy efficiency by displacing some of the need for electrical lighting and by admitting "free" solar heat that helps keep the indoors warm.

SKYLIGHTS IN SUMMER

Up to 90% of the energy required for electrical lighting is given off as heat—not light. By reducing the need for electrical lighting through the use of skylights, this heat source is effectively diminished. As a result, the air conditioning system works less and less energy is used in the summer. These reductions in the air conditioning load caused by less electrical lighting, along with the use of modern, thermally efficient skylights to reduce heat gain due to conduction, offset the summer "energy negatives" or solar heat and conductive heat gain. In addition, saving the "waste heat" from electrical lighting means saving the fossil fuels that are used to generate electricity at the power plant. Skylights thus are energy efficient in summer and winter.

SKYLIGHTS AND SAVINGS

An industrial-type building with skylights that cover up to 10% of the roof area can, with the proper selection and placement of the skylights, save annually the equivalent of up to 400,000 Btus (British thermal units) of energy per square foot of skylight compared to the same area of opaque roof insulated to current standards. The savings basically are the result of reduced energy costs for lighting and heating due to solar heat gain. These savings can help the homeowner, builder, or commercial building designer justify the cost of incorporating skylights in construction or remodeling plans.

As an example, a study was made on a proposed air-conditioned building 850 feet by 316 feet by 55 feet. The building, located in Jacksonville, Florida, was equipped with single-glazed skylights that covered about 3.6% of the roof area. Results indicated that the building could save annually the equivalent of 400,000 Btus of energy for each square foot of skylight for a total annual savings of 3.8 billion Btus. This represents some $35,000 worth of energy.

Several skylight manufacturers have at their disposal a computer program that helps builders and designers arrive at optimum skylight placement in order to maximize projected energy savings.

SOLAR ENERGY

The Earth receives solar radiation from the Sun, which is 93 million miles away. Just before the solar energy enters our atmosphere, the amount of energy available is called the solar constant, which is equal to 429 Btus/hour per square foot. This amount of energy is substantially reduced when it passes through the smog, haze, and cloud cover in the atmosphere.

All solar heating is achieved by what is called the greenhouse effect. Sunlight enters through windows, is absorbed by interior surfaces, and converted into heat. This heat is then reradiated outward, but does not pass back through the glass as readily as it entered, trapping a large percentage of the heat. A familiar example is a car parked in the sun. Through the greenhouse effect, interior temperatures can rise well above the outside air temperature.

There are two ways to gather and use the Sun's warmth: with active systems and with passive systems. Active solar heating systems use forced, heat-transfer mechanisms that include pumps and blowers. They usually consist of roof-mounted solar collector panels, fluid transfer components, storage tanks, and precise control systems. They do not offer direct lighting to the home's interior.

Passive solar systems are designed to heat, cool, and light buildings by using the natural light and heat of the Sun. The collector is the south face of the building itself. In the case of skylights, it is an opening in the south side of the roof.

DIRECT GAIN

Of all passive solar types, a direct gain system is the easiest to envision and construct. Sunlight enters living space through south-facing skylights or windows. It is absorbed by mass within the space—most commonly floors and walls—that can also serve structural functions. The distribution of heat and light is not critical to the operation of a direct gain system because the heat and light are used in the same area in which they are collected.

Skylights can be placed horizontally or at an angle on a sloping roof. Horizontal skylights can be problematical. They admit solar gain in the summer due to high sun angles, but permit minimal solar gain in the winter when it is most needed. Skylights are most beneficial when they are tilted steeply from the horizontal. The best angle places the greatest amount of glass surface toward the Sun year-round.

When using lower sloping skylights, reflectors can be added to increase the amount of radiation collected through the glass or aperture. Movable insulation should be placed over skylights to minimize heat losses. Make sure skylights are properly sealed and caulked.

Clerestories are south-facing vertical windows that project up from the roof surface. They can be placed anywhere on a roof. Clerestories should be located away from an interior storage wall so that direct sunlight hits low on the wall in winter. This distance should be roughly 1.5 times the height of the wall. Double glazing is recommended. Triple glazing should be used in severe climates. Single glazing can be used in mild climates if movable night insulation is provided to minimize heat loss. Summer shading can be provided by simple overhangs. For optimum light transfer, the ceiling adjacent to the clerestory should be light in color to reflect the sunlight.

Make sure trees and landscaping do not interfere with the Sun's light reaching your passive collector. Look for obstructions that may block sunlight today and in the future. If possible, remove trees that may block the Sun or, even better, move the skylight before it is installed. Think about how sunlight will enter the skylight in the winter when you most want the skylight's heat and light. Will deciduous trees drop their leaves and allow the Sun in through the skylight? Will the little tree below the Sun's arc quickly grow to block off light to your skylight?

SKYLIGHT GLAZINGS

Glass offers excellent selective transmission, good weatherability, and low thermal expansion. It is transparent and easily obtained. On the minus side, glass is expensive, heavy, breaks easily, and is difficult to install in larger sized panes.

Acrylic skylight material offers high optical clarity, strength, and weatherability. It is light-weight and easy to handle, impact resistant, and offers insulation properties similar to glass. The disadvantages include its higher cost, its being prone to surface abrasion, and its characteristics of expanding and contracting, which make it prone to sagging and even cracking.

Polycarbonate is similar to acrylic material and offers a very high impact strength. However, it scratches easily, becomes brittle, and changes color after prolonged exposure to the Sun.

Fiberglass-reinforced polyester is low in cost and easy to handle. It offers high strength and durability with coatings such as Tedlar and is available flat or with corrugations. Coatings reduce the amount of light and heat, however, and the product only has a medium life-span, which means it will have to be replaced in 5 to 10 years.

Polyester film is inexpensive and offers high surface hardness. Even so, it offers less light and heat transmittance than other materials and a medium life-span.

Polyethylene film is very inexpensive, lightweight, flexible, and easy to install. It offers good inner glazing properties. To its debit, polyethylene film has a short life-span, is not selective in the type of rays it collects from the Sun, and winds and temperature changes can cause it to sag.

Polyvinyl fluoride film offers excellent weatherability and strength with high solar transmittance. It is expensive, available only in thin film, and transmits more long light waves than other glazes.

All these glazes are used in solar windows and clerestories, but only acrylics (plexiglas and lucite), polycarbonates (lexan, Tuffack Twinwall, and Cyrolon SDP), and fiberglass-reinforced polyester (Lascolite, Filon and Tedlar, and Sunlight Premium II) are commonly used in skylights. Glass is not a common skylight material.

SKYLIGHT TYPES

There are many types of prefabricated skylights on the market. Shapes include round, oval, square, rectangular, triangular, and ridged, flat, domed, hipped, and barrel. The transparent surface can be plastic-glazed, clear, translucent, gray, or bronze. Skylight frames are made of wood, plastic, or metal. Custom-designed skylights also are available.

Self-flashing skylights (Fig. 5-1) have a built-in curb and flange for flashing and are used on roofs with less than a 3 in 12 pitch. The curb-mounted skylight (Fig. 5-2) is designed for roofs with a slope greater than 3 in 12. A curb and flashing must be built as the unit is installed.

Fig. 5-1. Self-flashing skylight.

Fig. 5-2. Curb-mounted skylight.

INSTALLING SKYLIGHTS

The tools you will need to install your skylight include a measuring tape, carpenter's square, hammer, framing nails, roofing nails, keyhole saw, roofing mastic, hand saw or power saw, tin snips, header lumber, framing lumber, and finish materials (Fig. 5-3). If you're installing a curb-mounted skylight, you'll also need a screwdriver, panhead wood screws (rust-resistant), aluminum flashing (curb height plus 6 inches), and 2 by 8 or larger dimension lumber.

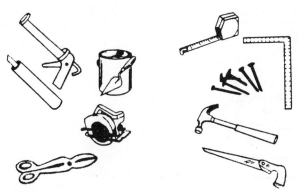

Fig. 5-3. Tools you'll need to install skylights.

Determine if your rafters are spaced 16 or 24 inches apart on centers. Rafter thickness sometimes varies depending on the age of the home. Therefore, spacing between your roof rafters may vary from Fig. 5-4. The frame and opening in the roof should be sized according to the inside dimensions of the skylight.

The first installation step for self-flashing and curb-mounted sky-lights is to locate the position for the skylight (Figs. 5-5 through 5-7). For an open-beam ceiling, drive a long nail from the inside of the house up through the roof at each corner of the planned skylight opening. Follow this same procedure for a conventional house, except drive the nails up from the attic or crawl space.

On the roof surface, locate the protruding nails. Remove the roofing material in the area bound by the four nails. After supporting the rafters that must be cut, make a hole in the roof surface. Except at the bottom of the opening, carefully lay back shingles and felt paper an additional 6 inches around the perimeter of the opening. Be careful not to cut through nails or staples when you cut the hole through the roof.

The third step is to install headers following the framing plans of the rafters. Rafter supports can now be removed.

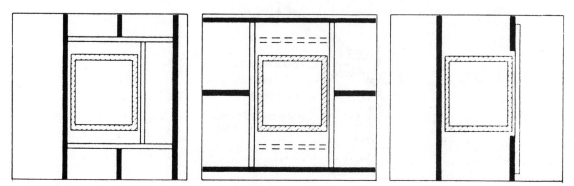

Fig. 5-4. Framing the skylight.

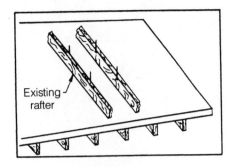

Existing rafter

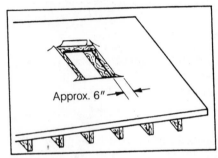

Approx. 6″

Fig. 5-5. Installing the skylight well.

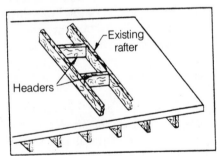

Existing rafter

Headers

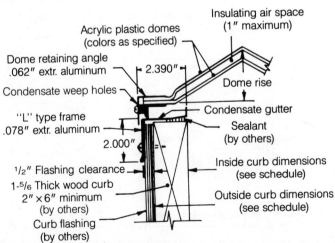

Insulating air space
(1″ maximum)

Acrylic plastic domes
(colors as specified)

Dome retaining angle
.062″ extr. aluminum

2.390″

Dome rise

Condensate weep holes

"L" type frame
.078″ extr. aluminum

Condensate gutter

Sealant
(by others)

2.000″

Inside curb dimensions
(see schedule)

¹/₂″ Flashing clearance

1-⁵/₆ Thick wood curb
2″ × 6″ minimum
(by others)

Outside curb dimensions
(see schedule)

Curb flashing
(by others)

Fig. 5-6. Cross section of skylight installation.

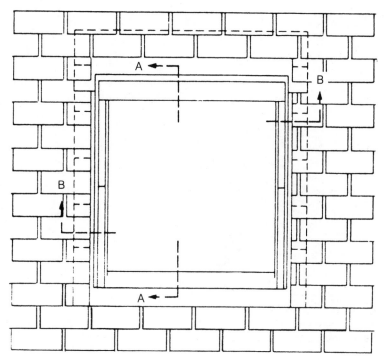

Fig. 5-7. The skylight opening.

Self-Flashing Skylight

If you are installing a self-flashing skylight on a sloping roof, the fourth step is to make sure the shingles are even with or a row beyond the bottom edge of the opening. Place two 1-inch wide by $^1/_8$-inch thick beads of roofing mastic 1 inch apart around the perimeter of the opening. Stay about an inch away from the edge (Fig. 5-8).

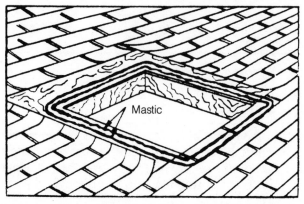

Fig. 5-8. Place two 1-inch wide by $^1/_8$-inch thick beads of roofing mastic an inch apart around the perimeter of the opening.

With skylight weep holes (arrows in Fig. 5-9) toward the bottom of the opening, center the skylight over the opening and secure it to the roof with roofing nails placed through punched holes in the flanges only. Place another bead of roofing mastic on top of the skylight flanges at the top and bottom sides. Then replace the shingles. Do not nail through the skylight flange. Mastic is adequate to seal the shingles (Fig. 5-10).

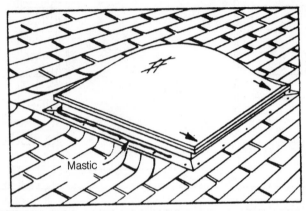

Mastic

Fig. 5-9. Center the skylight in the opening and secure it to the roof with nails.

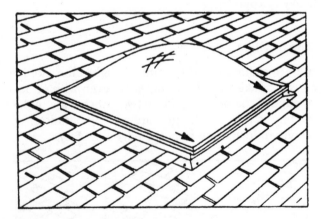

Fig. 5-10. Replace shingles and seal.

Curb-Mounted Skylight

The installation procedures for curb-mounted skylights are similar to those for self-flashing skylights. First, apply a coat of roofing mastic 1/8 inch thick and as wide as the curb lumber around the entire perimeter of the opening. Construct the wooden curb directly over the rafter frame opening (Fig. 5-11).

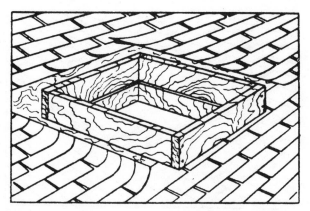

Fig. 5-11. Build the wood curb directly over the rafter frame opening.

Now fit aluminum sheet-metal flashing to the outside of the curb (Fig. 5-12). Flashing must go to the top of the curb and have a 3-inch flange around the base, except for a 6-inch flange on the top side. Seal the undersides and the top of the metal flanges with roofing mastic.

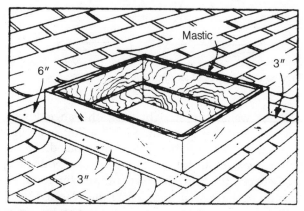

Fig. 5-12. Install metal flashing.

Install shingles and apply a ¹/₈-inch bead of roofing mastic around the entire perimeter of the top of the curb. With skylight weep holes (arrows in Fig. 5-13) toward the bottom of the opening, place the skylight on the curb and secure it with rust-resistant, panhead wood screws through pre-punched holes in the frame. Don't overtighten the screws.

The Skylight Well

Homes with conventional rather than cathedral ceilings must also have a skylight well in order for the light captured by the roof skylight to enter the rooms below the ceiling. Figure 5-14 illustrates three common

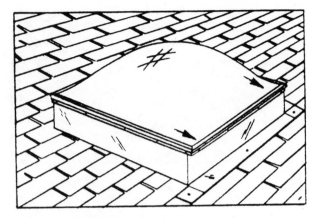

Fig. 5-13. Install shingles and secure the skylight.

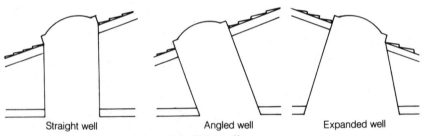

| Straight well | Angled well | Expanded well |

Fig. 5-14. Three common types of skylight wells.

types of skylight wells: the straight well, the angled well, and the expanded well. A well that is expanded will admit more light and disperse it so that the whole room is better illuminated. The appropriate design for your installation, however, depends on your needs and the relationships between the Sun, the skylight, and the room below.

To install the skylight well, first locate the planned location of the skylight and take measurements. Use walls and stairways as reference points. Go to the crawl space or attic and check your measurements. The ceiling opening may have to be shifted to one side so it can be aligned correctly with ceiling joists. Lay out the ceiling opening on the attic floor (Fig. 5-15).

Using a plumb bob, lay out the roof opening (depending on the style of light well) above the ceiling opening. Cut the hole in the ceiling as shown in Fig. 5-16. Brace across the ceiling joists as required. Install headers between the ceiling joists.

Finish framing the skylight well. The example shown in Fig. 5-17 is for a light well that is expanded to allow more light into the room. The well can be lined with the finishing materials of your choice. Be sure to insulate around the light well. If painting is required to finish off the light well, mask off the entire skylight to prevent paint splatters.

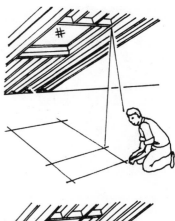

Fig. 5-15. Lay out the ceiling opening on the attic floor.

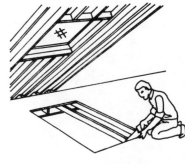

Fig. 5-16. Cut the hole in the ceiling.

Fig. 5-17. Finish framing the skylight well.

INSTALLING ROOF WINDOWS

A roof window is a rotary window that is installed in the roof. It opens to allow ventilation (Figs. 5-18 and 5-19). Installing a roof window is similar to installing a skylight, but there are enough differences to require separate installation instructions.

For comfortable operation by hand, the height from the finished floor level to the top of the window should be 6 feet 3 inches to 6 feet 9 inches (Fig. 5-20). As recommended, a horizontal soffit at the head (Fig. 5-20a) and a vertical lining at the sill (Fig. 5-20b) will give more headroom, better light distribution, and an attractive appearance. If possible, arrange the vertical lining (Fig. 5-20b) as shown with the heat source below the window to ensure a free flow of air over the glass (Fig.

Fig. 5-18. Roof windows can add living space to unused attic. (COURTESY OF VELUX-AMERICA INC.)

Fig. 5-19. The roof window offers natural lighting for efficient living. (COURTESY OF VELUX-AMERICA INC.)

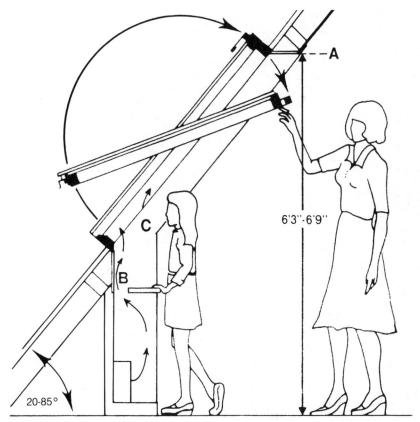

6'3"-6'9"

20-85°

Fig. 5-20. Using the roof window.

5-20c) and minimal condensation when the window is closed. Manual and power remote controls are available for out-of-reach windows.

Figure 5-4 illustrates three ways that rafters can be modified to accommodate roof windows. Before installation, the typical roof window must be disassembled. Separate the sash from the frame and remove the exterior cladding pieces from the frame (Fig. 5-21).

Install the frame in the roof. Screw the mounting brackets into the sheathing. Level the sill and take diagonal measurements to obtain squareness.

Install the sill flashing section (Fig. 5-22). It should be even with the front edge of the shingles. Nail the side pieces to the frame. See Figs. 5-23 and 5-24. Install the top flashing pieces. They should be interwoven with each layer of shingles. Then install the top-step flashing piece (Fig. 5-25). When necessary, cut the pieces as shown in the illustrations.

Replace exterior cladding (Fig. 5-26). Remember that pieces 2 and 4 are not interchangeable (Fig. 5-24). Install the head flashing section and interlock with the side cladding (Fig. 5-27). Replace the sash in the frame (Fig. 5-28).

Wood finishes should be retreated soon after installation.

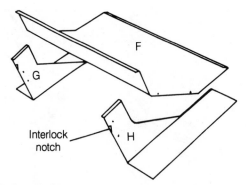

Fig. 5-21. Roof window flashing.

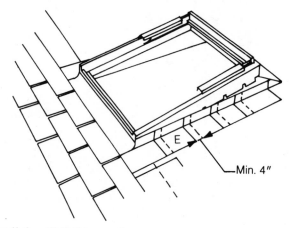

Fig. 5-22. Install the sill flashing section.

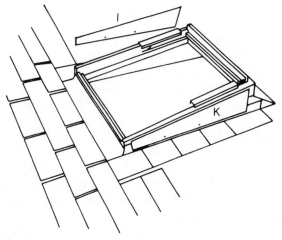

Fig. 5-23. Install side units.

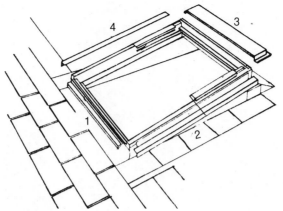

Fig. 5-24. Install casings.

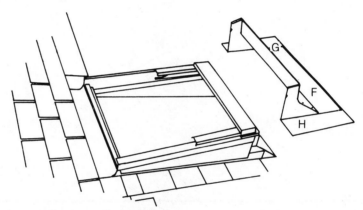

Fig. 5-25. Install top-step flashing pieces.

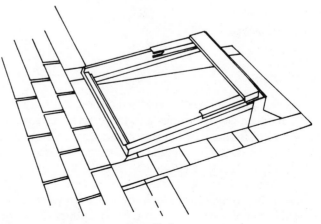

Fig. 5-26. Framing and flashing are installed.

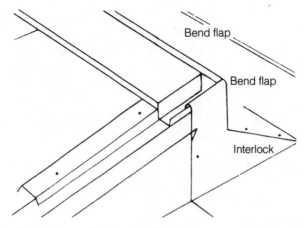

Bend flap

Bend flap

Interlock

Fig. 5-27. Details of top-step flashing installation.

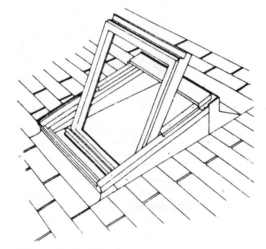

Fig. 5-28. The installed roof window.

SKYLIGHT CARE

To clean glass skylights and roof windows, use common household window cleaner. To clean acrylic domes and to remove electrostatic charges, wash with nonabrasive soap or detergent and water. Use your bare hand (no rags) to feel and dislodge any dirt that has hardened on the skylight or dome. A soft, clean cloth or sponge should be used only to carry water to the dome. After the dome has been thoroughly rinsed with clean water, dry the dome with a clean, damp chamois or cotton flannel. Rough or hard cloths should not be used because they will scratch a plastic dome.

Where water cannot be used freely, such as interior installations, the dome should first be dusted lightly, but not wiped, with a clean, soft cloth. Then wipe the dome carefully with a soft, wet chamois or cloth. The chamois or cloth should be rinsed off in clean water to keep it free of dirt that can scratch the finish.

To remove grease, oil, or roof caulking compounds, use kerosene or pure aliphatic naptha with no aromatic content. Solvents such as benzene acetone, fire-extinguisher fluid, carbon tetrachloride, dry cleaning fluid, lacquer thinners, and gasoline should not be used because they will attack the dome's acrylic surface. Scouring compounds should not be used.

If there is no great amount of scratching visible after cleaning the dome, it should be waxed with a high-quality paste or liquid wax that does not contain compounds that could scratch the dome. Waxing will improve the appearance of the dome by filling in minor scratches. Apply the wax in a thin, even coat and bring it to a high gloss by rubbing lightly with a dry, soft cloth such as cotton flannel. Avoid excessive rubbing with the dry cloth because it will cause scratches and build up an electrostatic charge that will attract dust particles to the dome's surface. Blotting the dome with a clean, damp cloth or chamois will remove the charge and any dust.

6

Selecting and Installing Solariums

UNTIL RECENTLY, SOLARIUMS OR SOLAR ROOMS WERE NOT PRACTICAL. Glassed-in rooms trapped the Sun's heat during warm days and increased the room's temperature to uncomfortable levels. On colder days, air inside the room transmitted its heat through the glass to the outside, making the room difficult to keep warm.

The past few years, however, have brought numerous technological advances in the design and production of the glass and seals. Though not as energy-efficient as a solid wall, solar glass can offer an R factor of 4—compared to a single glazing R factor of 0.9.

Solariums can be constructed by the do-it-yourselfer either from materials purchased at a building materials retailer or from a solarium dealer. In most cases, though, the homeowner has the solarium installed by an experienced contractor. The accidental breakage of just a couple panes of solar glass can eat up much of the savings earned by doing it yourself. Even so, knowing how the solarium is constructed will make you a smarter shopper and save you money.

Most solarium or greenhouse manufacturers offer idea books that will help you decide on the appropriate location and design for your addition. You will also want to talk with your banker regarding a second mortgage, interest rates, finance fees, repayment schedule, equity position, and whether or not they will finance such an addition if you do your own contracting.

A recent issue of *Remodeling Contractor* magazine estimated that a solarium or greenhouse addition to the typical home will return 100% on the homeowner's investment. This is a higher return than any other typical remodeling job. As a comparison, they estimated major kitchen remodeling as a 90% return on investment.

As you estimate the costs of your solarium, remember to include charges for additional wiring, electrical fixtures, plumbing, furniture, and other elements. They can easily add up and make a difference in how you finish your solarium.

Solariums or greenhouses can be added as a new room or onto any room in your home: kitchen, living room, dining room, family room, recreation room, or even a bathroom if designed properly. The hardest part is deciding where you want to place your solarium. Consider visibility, solar radiation, privacy, architecture, trees, and your own living style.

PLANNING YOUR SOLARIUM

To make certain that your solarium or greenhouse fits properly against your home, take on-site measurements and double check them for accuracy. Making the correct elevation measurements is most important, since they are more difficult (Figs. 6-1 through 6-3).

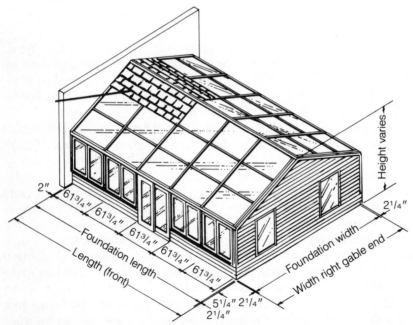

Fig. 6-1. Planning your full solarium. (COURTESY OF FOUR SEASONS SOLAR PRODUCTS CORP.)

To plan your solarium, first draw a sketch of the side elevation so that all related dimensions can be recorded. Use drafting or graph paper to ensure an accurate scale and measurements. Use a nail or marker to

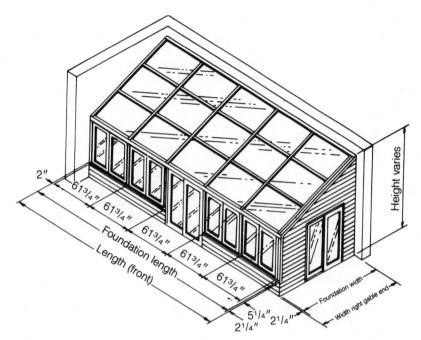

Fig. 6-2. Attached solarium. (COURTESY OF FOUR SEASONS SOLAR PRODUCTS CORP.)

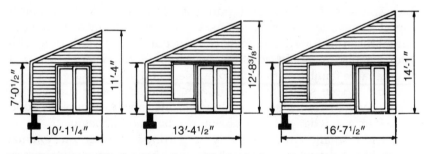

Fig. 6-3. Typical side elevations for attached solariums. (COURTESY OF FOUR SEASONS SOLAR PRODUCTS CORP.)

mark the inside floor elevation as 0'0" on the outside wall of the house. Every other elevation will be measured relative to this point. Higher points will be indicated in positive numbers above 0'0" and lower points will be written as negative numbers. Complete all elevation measurements as shown in Figs. 6-4 and 6-5.

Mark the location of doors and windows on the elevation plan as an aid in planning your layout. Be careful that doors are placed in the correct location and that they will have sufficient headroom.

Verify your dimensions, make a final floor plan, and then you're ready to order your solarium kit or components and begin construction.

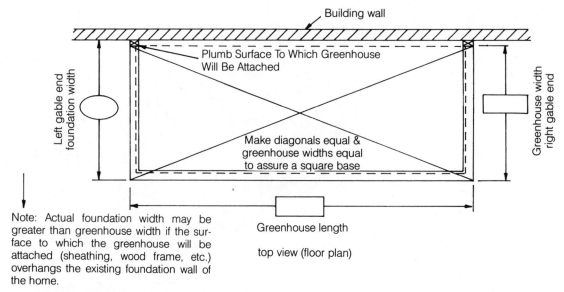

Note: Actual foundation width may be greater than greenhouse width if the surface to which the greenhouse will be attached (sheathing, wood frame, etc.) overhangs the existing foundation wall of the home.

Fig. 6-4. Complete your own plans using graph paper. (COURTESY OF FOUR SEASONS SOLAR PRODUCTS CORP.)

CONSTRUCTION

Once you've selected your solarium components or kit, take time to inspect all materials before beginning construction. A cracked pane or a frame broken in transit can delay construction unless you can quickly order a replacement. In addition, by verifying all materials you will become more familiar with each component and actually save construction time. If your solarium is in kit form, especially make sure you are aware of what isn't included, such as glazing tape, fasteners, or adhesives. Purchase what you need so you will be ready to begin.

There are many ways of properly supporting your solarium. You may wish to match the exterior of your home by using a basewall with matching siding or exterior finish. The interior finish of the basewall should be decorated as desired and may also be used to house heating ducts, plumbing and electrical lines. Refer to Fig. 6-6 for suggestions on foundation construction.

Insulate the foundation below ground level either inside or outside as appropriate. Use styrofoam, fiberglass, or other insulation. The sill may be mounted directly on a masonry foundation or basewall or on a 2-by-6 or 2-by-8 wooden sill over masonry to provide a smooth, level surface. Use only pressure-treated lumber and weatherproof caulking. Make sure that the foundation and basewall are plumb, level, and square to ensure an accurate installation.

Then install the flashing to give a finished appearance to the sill that will drain water away from the basewall. Flashing is best held in place only by caulking so that there are no leaks around fasteners.

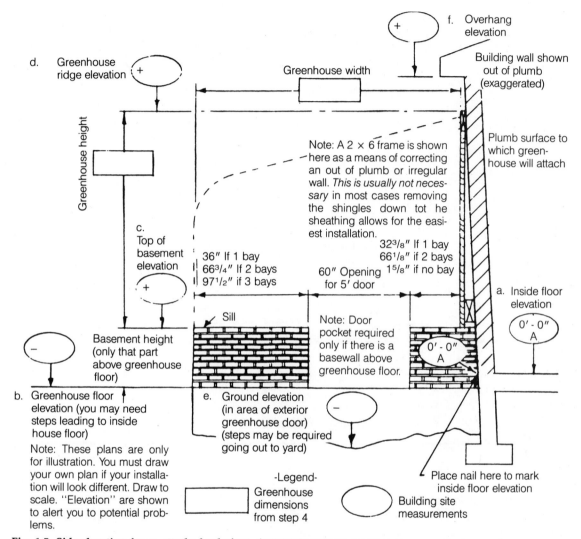

d.   Greenhouse ridge elevation ⊕

Greenhouse width

f.   Overhang elevation ⊕

Building wall shown out of plumb (exaggerated)

Greenhouse height

Plumb surface to which green-house will attach

Note: A 2 × 6 frame is shown here as a means of correcting an out of plumb or irregular wall. *This is usually not necessary* in most cases removing the shingles down tot he sheathing allows for the easiest installation.

c.   Top of basement elevation ⊕

36" If 1 bay
66³/₄" If 2 bays
97¹/₂" if 3 bays

32³/₈" If 1 bay
66¹/₈" if 2 bays
1⁵/₈" if no bay

60" Opening for 5' door

a.   Inside floor elevation

0' - 0"
A

⊖

Basement height (only that part above greenhouse floor)

Sill

Note: Door pocket required only if there is a basewall above greenhouse floor.

0' - 0"
A

b.   Greenhouse floor elevation (you may need steps leading to inside house floor)

Note: These plans are only for illustration. You must draw your own plan if your installation will look different. Draw to scale. "Elevation" are shown to alert you to potential problems.

e.   Ground elevation (in area of exterior greenhouse door) (steps may be required going out to yard)

⊖

-Legend-

Greenhouse dimensions from step 4

Building site measurements

Place nail here to mark inside floor elevation

Fig. 6-5. Side elevation for an attached solarium. (COURTESY OF FOUR SEASONS SOLAR PRODUCTS CORP.)

Next, install ¹/₄-inch lag bolts in the sill. Carefully caulk and install the sill end plates and sill flashing. The sill flashing can be installed with a 6 inch overlap and caulking in between, or with a butt joint on top of thin aluminum flashing.

Make any cutouts for the door opening area, as shown in Fig. 6-7. Once the entire sill perimeter is laid out and all door cut-outs made, the sill can be fastened to the foundation using lag bolts or a masonry anchor. Caulk the sill flashing in place.

A smooth and plumb vertical surface is required for installing the solarium. A smooth brick or wood surface is usually sufficient, but a rough shingle or other uneven surface must be removed down to the

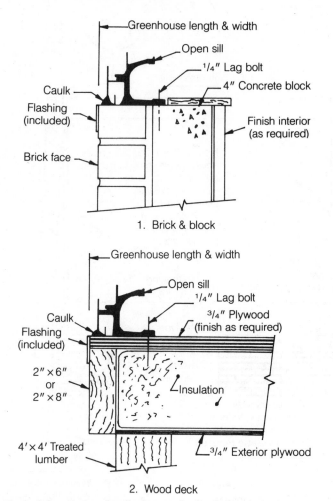

Fig. 6-6. Typical foundation details for attached solariums. (COURTESY OF FOUR SEASONS SOLAR PRODUCTS CORP.)

sheathing. Once exact locations of the wall bar and ridge are established, install them using steel nails and ridge clips as shown in Fig. 6-8.

SOLARIUM FRAMING

The frame or glazing bars are installed next. The distance between glazing bars depends on the design of your solarium, but must be exactly measured. Slide the glazing bar over the ridge clip, then insert the glazing bar into the sill. Make sure all components are plumb, true, and exactly on center, then fasten the glazing bar into place with sheet metal screws.

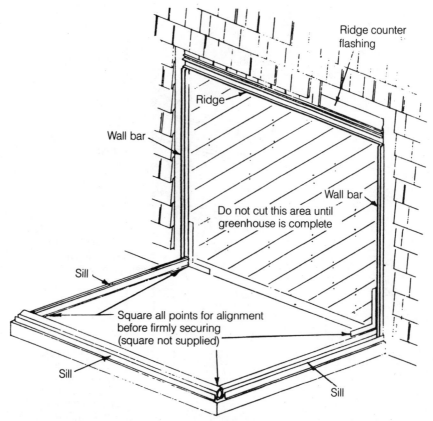

Ridge counter flashing

Ridge

Wall bar

Wall bar

Do not cut this area until greenhouse is complete

Sill

Square all points for alignment before firmly securing (square not supplied)

Sill

Sill

Fig. 6-7. Preparing the foundation and wall site. (COURTESY OF FOUR SEASONS SOLAR PRODUCTS CORP.)

Next, install the cross-members or muntins (Fig. 6-9). Refer to your plans for the exact location of each muntin. Then step back and make sure all muntins are aligned and look good. Don't install the gable muntins until the gable end is complete.

Install the gable ends and flashing, the glazing bar, and related components as shown in Fig. 6-10 and 6-11. Make sure that each gable end bar is perfectly plumb and evenly-spaced before securing it into place.

Once your solarium frame is in place, install the power ventilation blower, shutter, and casing (Fig. 6-12) per the manufacturer's instructions. You may need to have an electrician assist in the installation to conform to code.

INSTALLING SOLARIUM DOORS AND WINDOWS

Your door may be installed against the house wall or within two bays in either the front or gable end. The door is installed into a door jamb built

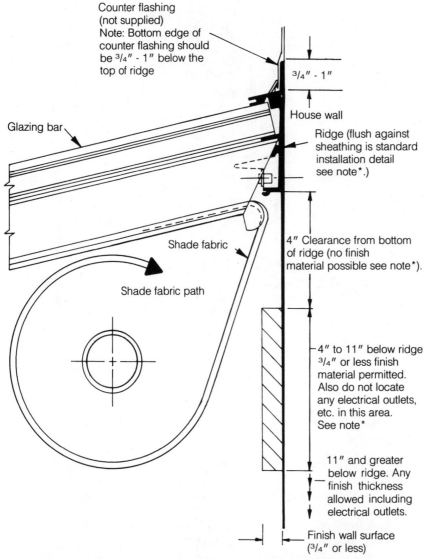

Counter flashing
(not supplied)
Note: Bottom edge of
counter flashing should
be 3/4" - 1" below the
top of ridge

3/4" - 1"

House wall

Glazing bar

Ridge (flush against
sheathing is standard
installation detail
see note*.)

Shade fabric

4" Clearance from bottom
of ridge (no finish
material possible see note*).

Shade fabric path

4" to 11" below ridge
3/4" or less finish
material permitted.
Also do not locate
any electrical outlets,
etc. in this area.
See note*

11" and greater
below ridge. Any
finish thickness
allowed including
electrical outlets.

Finish wall surface
(3/4" or less)

Fig. 6-8. Installing the glazing bar against the ridge. (COURTESY OF FOUR SEASONS SOLAR PRODUCTS CORP.)

during construction. Install sealer around the jamb, then place the door within the jamb. Check for clearance and seal before continuing. Shim the door frame and sill until the door is tight against the frame and plumb. Remember that the door must be perfectly square in order to operate properly.

Once the door is perfectly placed, drill three 1/8-inch holes through each door frame side into the glazing bar and install the screws. Make any final adjustments, add shims and sill trim to the bottom of the door, drill 1/8-inch holes, and install with screws.

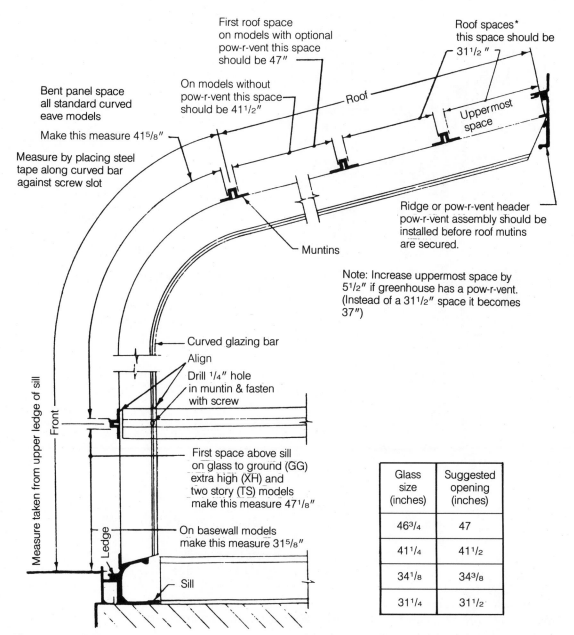

Fig. 6-9. Installing cross-members or muntins. (COURTESY OF FOUR SEASONS SOLAR PRODUCTS CORP.)

Windows or glazing for your solarium require time and patience to install. Taking your time and doing it right the first time, however, will actually save you time. Figures 6-13 and 6-14 illustrate how glazing is installed in one brand of solarium; yours may differ, but the procedures are basically the same.

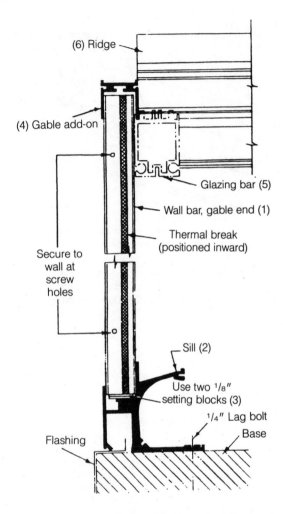

(6) Ridge

(4) Gable add-on

Secure to
wall at
screw
holes

Glazing bar (5)

Wall bar, gable end (1)

Thermal break
(positioned inward)

Sill (2)

Use two 1/8"
setting blocks (3)

1/4" Lag bolt

Base

Flashing

Fig. 6-10. Installing a wall bar vent. (COURTESY OF FOUR SEASONS SOLAR PRODUCTS CORP.)

First, apply glazing tape on the glazing bars, sill, muntin caps, and muntins. Then apply a 1-inch bead of caulk on the glazing cord and glazing tape prior to installing the first glass panel. Insert the glazing cord in the glazing bar caps. Install glazing in the bay closest to the ridge. Continue installing glazing horizontally until the roof is complete.

Assemble the curved acrylic glazing panel and install the upper edge of the panel onto the muntin, securing it into place. Install the front glazing panels in the same manner.

In some cases, the glazing panels are clipped into place, while others are screwed or snapped. Most glazing schemes have a beauty bar that covers the edge of the glazing within the frame. Make sure you uniformly tighten all glazing screws to equalize stress and minimize damage. Keep in mind that replacing a broken curved glazing panel can cost over $200.

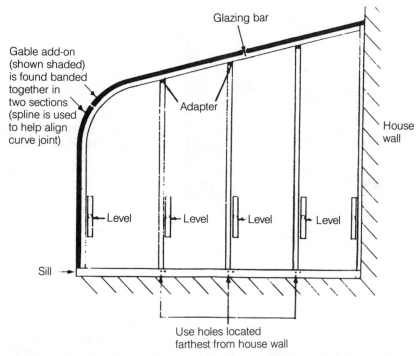

Fig. 6-11. Make sure all glazing bars are perfectly vertical. (COURTESY OF FOUR SEA-SONS SOLAR PRODUCTS CORP.)

Finally, install glazing panels in the gable ends in the same manner. In some cases, you will need to add a shim to ensure a snug fit. If further adjustment is required, move the gable end glazing bars, drill through the sill, and reattach. Shim behind the wall bar as required.

SOLVING SOLARIUM PROBLEMS

Even the most meticulous installation can have a few problems. However, in most cases, the remedy is simple. If water leaks into your solarium from behind the ridge, check the installation of the counter flashing and caulking (Fig. 6-15). If water is leaking in from the roof area, check the cross muntins and apply a 1/16-inch bead of clear silicone across all roof muntins. If water leaks in around a screw, remove the screw and fill the screw hole with silicone before replacing the screw. If water leaks around an awning window, check the caulking on the cross muntin above the window. If you find water leaking in at the sill, check the sill flashing and caulking, or remove the gable corner plate and make sure it is properly caulked, or review all caulking. If the sill leaks where it is attached to the wall, remove the sill cover plate and make sure the caulking at the end of the sill is unbroken. If no gable end exists, make certain that the flexible gable flashing is properly installed.

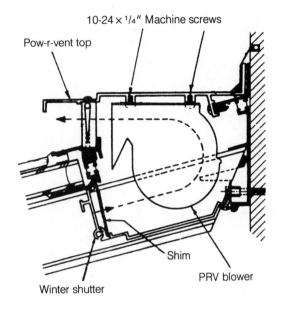

10-24 × ¼″ Machine screws

Pow-r-vent top

Shim

PRV blower

Winter shutter

Fig. 6-12. Installing a typical power vent blower assembly. (COURTESY OF FOUR SEASONS SOLAR PRODUCTS CORP.)

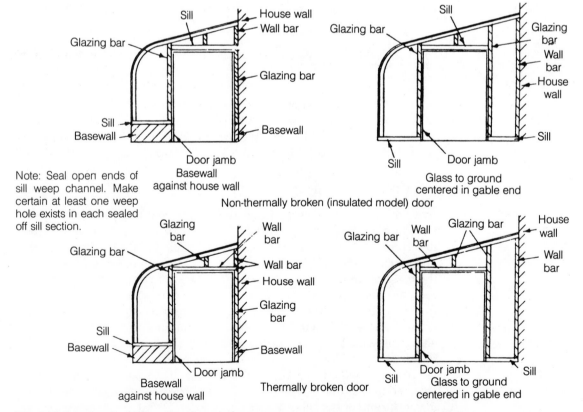

Sill

House wall

Wall bar

Glazing bar

Glazing bar

Sill

Basewall

Basewall

Door jamb

Basewall against house wall

Note: Seal open ends of sill weep channel. Make certain at least one weep hole exists in each sealed off sill section.

Non-thermally broken (insulated model) door

Sill

Glazing bar

Glazing bar

Wall bar

House wall

Sill

Door jamb

Sill

Glass to ground centered in gable end

Glazing bar

Glazing bar

Wall bar

Wall bar

House wall

Glazing bar

Sill

Basewall

Basewall

Door jamb

Basewall against house wall

Thermally broken door

Glazing bar

Wall bar

Glazing bar

House wall

Wall bar

Door jamb

Sill

Glass to ground centered in gable end

Fig. 6-13. Framing the sliding glass door. (COURTESY OF FOUR SEASONS SOLAR PRODUCTS CORP.)

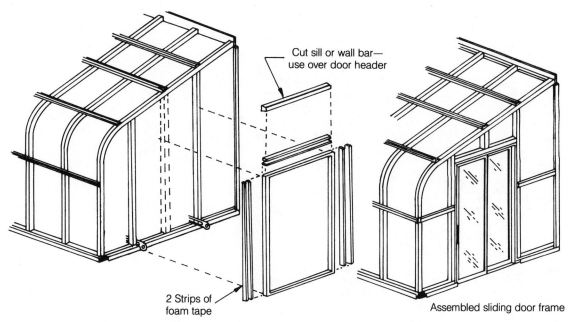

Cut sill or wall bar—
use over door header

2 Strips of
foam tape

Assembled sliding door frame

Fig. 6-14. Installing the sliding glass door in the solarium end. (COURTESY OF FOUR SEASONS SOLAR PRODUCTS CORP.)

If a sliding door or screen binds, first clear the track of debris. If this doesn't solve the problem, adjust the door and screen. Once done, spray the track with lubricant to reduce friction. If a window crank is too tight, spray silicone on the handle mechanism and at the lower edge of the window.

For more serious problems, contact your solarium contractor, retailer, or manufacturer. Keep all installation manuals, receipts, contracts, warranties, and related paperwork in a safe and accessible location in case you must refer to it later or pass it on to the next homeowner.

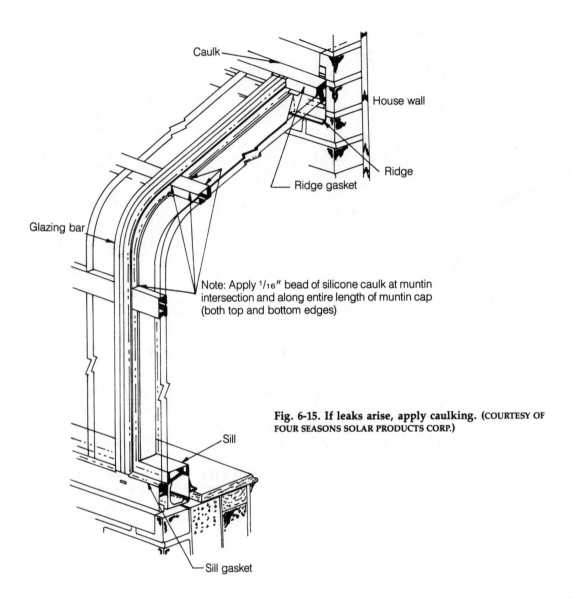

Caulk

House wall

Ridge

Ridge gasket

Glazing bar

Note: Apply $1/16''$ bead of silicone caulk at muntin intersection and along entire length of muntin cap (both top and bottom edges)

Fig. 6-15. If leaks arise, apply caulking. (COURTESY OF FOUR SEASONS SOLAR PRODUCTS CORP.)

Sill

Sill gasket

7

Painting and Finishing Barriers

DOORS, WINDOWS, AND SKYLIGHTS SHOULD BE PAINTED WITH A QUALITY finish to extend their life and attractiveness (Fig. 7-1). Many woods and wood products are used in manufactured barriers. These wooden surfaces can be finished quite effectively by several methods. Painting, which totally obscures the wood grain, is used to achieve a particular color decor (Fig. 7-2). Penetrating-type preservatives and pigmented stains permit some or all of the wood grain and texture to show, and they provide a special color effect and a natural or rustic appearance (Fig. 7-3). The type of finish, painted or natural, often depends on the wood to be finished.

WORKING WITH WOODS

Wooden surfaces that shrink and swell the least are best for painting. For this reason, vertical- or edge-grained surfaces are far better than the flat-grained surface of any species. Also, because the swelling of wood depends on its density, low-density species are preferred over high-density species.

Table 7-1 illustrates the characteristics of woods for painting and finishing. The woods are rated by ease of painting. Group I woods are easiest to paint and repaint while Group V woods are more difficult. Most door, window, and skylight frames are made from softwoods. Some exterior doors and better window sashes are made of hardwoods.

The properties of wood that detract from its paintability do not necessarily affect the finishing of such boards naturally with penetrating preservatives and stains. These finishes penetrate into the wood without

Fig. 7-1. Doors can be decorative. (COURTESY OF E. A. NORD CO.)

forming a continuous film on the surface. They will not blister, crack, or peel even if excessive moisture penetrates into the wood. One way to further improve the performance of penetrating finishes is to leave the surface rough sawn. Allowing the high-density, flat-grained surfaces of lumber and plywood to weather several months also roughens the surfaces and improves them for staining. Rough-textured surfaces absorb more of the preservative and stain, ensuring a more durable finish.

NATURAL WOOD FINISHING

The simplest of natural wood finishes is natural weathering. Without paint or treatment of any kind, wooden surfaces change in color and texture in a few months or years. The surfaces may stay almost unaltered for a long time if the wood does not decay. Generally, the dark-colored woods (Table 7-1) become lighter and the light-colored woods become

Fig. 7-2. The unfinished door can easily be painted to match your home's colors and mood. (COURTESY OF E. A. NORD CO.)

darker. As weathering continues, all woods become gray from the degradation of the wood cells at the surface. Unfinished wood will wear away at the rate of about ¹/₄ inch in 100 years.

The appearance of weathered wood is affected by dark-colored spores and mycelia of fungi or mildew on the surface, which give the wood a dark gray, blotchy, and unsightly appearance. Highly-colored wood extractives in such species as western red cedar and redwood also influence the color of weathered wood. The dark brown color may persist for a long time in areas not exposed to the Sun and where extractives are not removed by rain, such as in a sheltered doorway.

With naturally weathered wood, it is important to avoid the unsightly effect of rusting nails. Iron nails rust rapidly and produce a severe brown or black discoloration on the wood. Thus, only aluminum or stainless steel nails should be used for natural finishes.

Fig. 7-3. A clear finish can enhance the wood grain. (COURTESY OF E. A. NORD CO.)

WATER-REPELLENT PRESERVATIVES

The natural weathering of wood may be modified by treating it with water-repellent finishes that contain a preservative, usually pentachlorophenol or penta, a small amount of resin, and a very small amount of a water repellent that frequently is wax or wax-like in nature. The treatment, which penetrates the surface, retards the growth of mildew, prevents water from staining the ends of boards, reduces warping, and protects species that have a low natural resistance to decay. A clear, golden tan color can be achieved on smooth or rough-sawn western red cedar and redwood by using a water-repellent finish.

The preservative solution can be easily applied by dipping, brushing, or spraying. During the first two or three years, the finish may have to be applied every year or so. After weathering reaches a uniform color, the treatments are more durable and need to be reapplied only when the surface becomes unevenly colored.

Table 7-1. Characteristics of Wood for Painting and Finishing.

Wood	Ease of keeping well-painted I—easiest V—most exacting[1]	Weathering		Appearance	
		Resistance to cupping 1—best 4—worst	Conspicuousness of checking 1—least 2—most	Color of heartwood (sapwood is always light)	Degree of figure on flat-grained surface
Softwoods					
Cedar:					
Alaska	I	1	1	yellow	faint
California incense	I			brown	faint
Port-Orford	I		1	cream	faint
Western redcedar	I	1	1	brown	distinct
White	I	1		light brown	distinct
Cypress	I	1	1	light brown	strong
Redwood	I	1	1	dark brown	distinct
Pine:					
Eastern white	II	2	2	cream	faint
Sugar	II	2	2	cream	faint
Western white	II	2	2	cream	faint
Ponderosa	III	2	2	cream	distinct
Fir, commercial white	III	2	2	white	faint
Hemlock	III	2	2	pale brown	faint
Spruce	III	2	2	white	faint
Douglas fir (lumber and plywood)	IV	2	2	pale red	strong
Larch	IV	2	2	brown	strong
Pine:					
Norway	IV	2	2	light brown	distinct
Southern (lumber and plywood)	IV	2	2	light brown	strong
Tamarack	IV	2	2	brown	strong
Hardwoods					
Alder	III			pale brown	faint
Aspen	III	2	1	pale brown	faint
Basswood	III	2	2	cream	faint
Cottonwood	III	4	2	white	faint
Magnolia	III	2		pale brown	faint
Poplar	III	2	1	pale brown	faint
Beech	IV	4	2	pale brown	faint
Birch	IV	4	2	light brown	faint
Gum	IV	4	2	brown	faint
Maple	IV	4	2	light brown	faint
Sycamore	IV			pale brown	faint
Cherry	IV			brown	faint
Ash	V or III	4	2	light brown	distinct
Butternut	V or III			light brown	faint
Chestnut	V or III	3	2	light brown	distinct
Walnut	V or III	3	2	dark brown	distinct
Elm	V or IV	4	2	brown	distinct
Hickory	V or IV	4	2	light brown	distinct
Oak, white	V or IV	4	2	brown	distinct
Oak, red	V or IV	4	2	brown	distinct

[1]Woods ranked in group V for *ease of keeping well-painted* are hardwoods with large pores that need filling with wood filler for durable painting. When so filled before painting, the second classification recorded in the table applies.

The pigmented penetrating stains are semitransparent and permit much of the grain pattern to show through. They penetrate into the wood without forming a continuous film on the surface and will not blister, crack, or peel even if excessive moisture enters the wood (Fig. 7-4). Penetrating stains are suitable for both smooth and rough-textured surfaces. Their performance is markedly improved, though, if applied to rough-sawn, weathered, or rough-textured wood. They are especially effective on lumber and plywood that does not hold paint well, such as the flat-grained surfaces of dense species (Table 7-1). One coat of penetrating stain applied to a smooth surface may last only 2 to 4 years, but the second application, applied after the surface has been roughened by weathering, can last 8 to 10 years. A finish life of close to 10 years can be achieved initially by applying two coats of stain to rough-sawn surfaces.

SURFACE PREPARATION

Preparation of the surface—cleaning and patching—may take a lot of time. Even the best paint will not adhere well to an excessively dirty or greasy surface, or hide large cracks or scratches. Scrape away peeling paint and cover it on barriers in homes where original paints may have had a lead base. Such paints are a hazard, especially to children who nat-

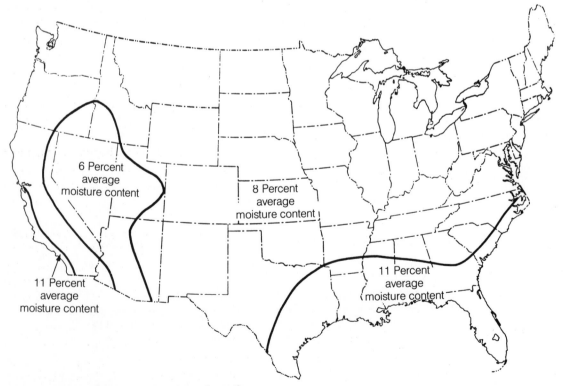

Fig. 7-4. Wood moisture content across the nation.

urally want to put these chips in their mouths and eat them, which can be very harmful or even fatal.

A surface that is to be painted should be firm, smooth, and clean. If you are using oil-based paint, the surface must also be completely dry. If necessary, latex or water-based paint can be applied to a damp but not wet surface. Ideal conditions, though, are dry surfaces. Check the paint can label for additional instructions for preparing the surface to be painted.

Doors and windows that get a great deal of "hand traffic" should be cleaned of grease and grime before painting. Skylights in the kitchen that may catch cooking grease should be stripped of any buildup.

Wooden surfaces in window sashes, doors, and skylight frames should not contain resinous knots or pitch streaks. If they do, clean the knots and streaks with turpentine and seal with a good knot sealer. The knot sealer will seal in oily extractives and reduce the staining and cracking of the paint in the knot area. If there are any bare spots in the wood, prime them with an undercoating.

To prevent future staining by rusty nails, set nailheads below the surface, prime them, and caulk holes. Loose wood should be fastened with galvanized nails. Prime and caulk all cracks. Sand the area smooth after the compound dries.

Remove all rough, loose, flaking, and blistering paint on surfaces that you are repainting. Spot prime bare spots. Where the cracking or blistering of the old paint extends over a large area, remove all old paint down to bare wood. Prime and repaint the old surface as you would a new wooden surface. Sand or feather the edges of the tight old paint before repainting.

Smooth any rough spots in the wood with sandpaper or another abrasive. Before applying paint, wipe off any dust or residue left on the surface from cleaning or surface preparation.

Old paint may be removed by sanding, scraping, burning, or using a chemical paint remover. Sanding is the cheapest and most difficult method. Chemical paint removers are practical only on small areas such as window sashes and detail work on door panels. Burning is not recommended.

New galvanized steel surfaces should weather for about 6 months before being painted. If earlier painting is necessary, wash the surface with a very mild, diluted acid such as vinegar or a commercially available compound, and rinse it thoroughly. This will remove any manufacturing residue and stain inhibitors. Apply a special metallic zinc dust primer or other specially formulated primer before painting.

Rust and loose paint can usually be removed from old surfaces with sandpaper or with a stiff wire brush. Chipping may be necessary in severe cases. Chemical rust removers are also available. Oil and grease may be removed with a solvent such as mineral spirits. Rinse the surface thoroughly.

SELECTING PAINT

Consider whether you need an exterior (exposed to weather) or interior paint. Consider the surface you are painting: wood, metal, or masonry. Some paints can be used for any surface, but most are formulated for one particular surface material. The condition of the surface is also important. Old chalky surfaces, for example, are not generally a sound base for latex or water-based paints.

Consider any special requirements. Non-chalking paint may be best where chalk runoff would discolor adjacent brick or stone surfaces that are difficult to clean. If mildew is a problem, mildew-resistant paints should be purchased. Tables 7-2 and 7-3 will help you decide the appropriate paints for interior and exterior doors, windows, skylights, and other home applications. For a more specific selection, consult your paint dealer.

TYPES OF PAINT

Paint may be categorized as solvent-thinned or water-thinned. Solvent-thinned paints are most commonly oil-based paints, but some specialty coatings such as catalyzed epoxies, polyesters, and urethanes are also solvent-thinned. They are not oil-based paints. Enamels made with a varnish or resin base instead of linseed oil are included under oil paints. Water-thinned paints are most commonly latex paints, but there are also nonlatex paints that are water-thinned.

Oil-based paints are very durable, highly resistant to stain and damage, able to withstand frequent scrubbings, and give good one-coat coverage.

Many latex paints are advertised as having similar properties. The main advantages to latex are easier application, faster drying, and simpler cleanup. The brushes, rollers, and other equipment used with latex paint can be easily cleaned with soap and water.

Paints usually come in three finishes: gloss, semigloss, and flat. Glossy finishes look shiny and clean easily. Flat finishes reduce glare, but they become dirty more readily. Semigloss finishes have properties of both glossy and flat finishes. Both oil-based and latex paints are available in gloss, semigloss, and flat finishes.

Because enamel is durable and easy to clean, semigloss or full-gloss enamel is recommended for doors, window sashes, and many walls. Flat paint is generally used for the walls of living rooms, dining rooms, and other nonwork and nonplay rooms.

Penetrating sealers are available as finishes for paneling and molding. They are easy to apply and penetrate into the surface with little buildup. A sealer avoids the high gloss finish that some people don't like.

House paint is the commercial term for exterior paints. Generally, it refers to paint applied to siding and other large exterior wall surfaces.

Table 7-2. Exterior Paint Selection Chart.

Surface	Aluminum paint	Asphalt emulsion	Awning paint	Cement-based paint	House paint (oil)	House paint (latex)	Metal primer	Porch-and-deck enamel	Primer or undercoater	Roof cement or coating	Spar varnish	Transparent sealer	Trim-and-trellis paint	Water repellent preservative	Penetrating wood stain (latex or oil)
Masonry															
Asbestos cement					X•	X			X						
Brick	X			X	X•	X			X				X		
Cement and cinder block	X			X	X•	X			X				X		
Cement porch floor						X		X	X						
Stucco	X			X	X•	X			X				X		
Metal															
Aluminum windows	X				X•	X•	X						X•		
Galvanized surfaces	X•				X•	X•	X						X•		
Iron surfaces	X•				X•	X•	X		X				X•		
Siding (metal)	X•				X•	X•	X•						X•		
Steel windows and doors	X•				X•	X•	X						X•		
Wood															
Frame windows	X				X•	X•			X				X•		X
Natural siding and trim												X			X
Porch floor								X							X
Shingle roof														X	X
Shutters and other trim					X•	X•			X				X•		X
Siding					X•	X•			X						X
Miscellaneous															
Canvas awnings			X												
Coal tar felt roof		X								X					

[1]X = Paint choice and • = Primer or sealer may be required, check container label.

Trim paint is usually used for baseboards, windowsills, trim, and other jobs. There are paints specifically formulated for nearly every requirement, such as rust-preventive paint for metal.

Because wooden trim is usually treated with a water-repellent preservative before finishing, any form of latex or oil-based paint or stain can be used. Latex trim enamels are good choices for trim, windows, shutters, and doors. Their properties include rapid drying, high gloss, good color and color retention, and good durability. Regular house paint may not retain its gloss as long. Chalking paints should be avoided whenever there is concern about discoloration of adjacent surfaces.

Table 7-3. Interior Paint Selection Chart.

Surface	Alkali resistant enamel	Alkyd exterior masonry paint	Alkyd flat enamel	Alkyd floor enamel	Alkyd glossy enamel	Alkyd semigloss enamel	Epoxy enamel (opaque)	Epoxy finish (clear)	Lacquer	Latex exterior masonry paint	Latex flat wall paint	Latex floor enamel	Latex glossy enamel	Latex semigloss enamel	Pigmented wiping stain	Portland cement masonry paint	Portland cement metal paint	Shellac	Urethane enamel (opaque)	Urethane finish (clear)	Varnish
Masonry Brick	X 11	X 11	X 8,11		X 8,11	X 8,11	X 11,7			X 11	X 8,11		X 8,11	X 8,11					X 11,7		
Cement block	X 11		X 4,7		X 11	X 4,7	X 4,7				X 4,7		X 4,7	X 4,7		X 11			X 11,7		
Ceramic tile flooring				X 11			X 11					X 11							X 11		
Concrete	X 11		X 4,11	X 11	X 4,11	X 4,11	X 11				X 4,11	X 11	X 4,11	X 4,11		X 11			X 11		
Concrete flooring	X 11			X 11			X 11					X 11							X 11		
Drywall			X 6		X 6	X 6	X 6,11				X 6,11		X 6	X 6					X 6,11		
Plaster			X 6,2		X 6,2	X 6,2	X 6,11				X 6,11		X 6	X 6					X 6,11		
Metal Aluminum			X 1		X 1	X 1	X 1				X 1		X 1	X 1					X 1		
Galvanized steel			X 14		X 14	X 14	X 14				X 14		X 14	X 14		X 10	X 10		X 14		
Iron and steel			X 1,5		X 1,5	X 1,5	X 1,11				X 1,5		X 1,5	X 1,5		X 10	X 10		X 14		
Steel flooring				X 11			X 11									X 10	X 10		X 11		
Wood Flooring				X 11			X 11	X 11	X 11			X 11			X 13,12			X 11	X 11	X 11	X 13,12
Trim and paneling			X 3		X 3	X 3	X 3,11	X 11	X 11		X 3		X 3	X 3	X 13,12			X 11	X 3,11	X 11	X 13,12
Miscellaneous `Acoustical tile			X 2								X 11										
Vinyl wallcovering, smooth, with design			X 11		X 11	X 11					X 11		X 11	X 11							
Vinyl wallcovering, smooth, without design					X 11	X 11					X 11										
Vinyl wallcovering, textured			X 9,11		X 9,11	X 9,11					X 11										
Wallpaper			X 6,2		X 6,2	X 6,2					X 6,2		X 6,2	X 6,2							

`X = Paint choice and numbers = Primer choice.

If when painting windows and doors you must also paint wooden siding, either latex or oil-based house paint may be used. An oil-based primer is recommended for resinous woods, such as pine, and those that tend to bleed, such as redwood and western red cedar. Penetrating semi-transparent stains are preferred by many homeowners who want to preserve the beauty of wood (Fig. 7-5).

Exterior latex masonry paint is a standard paint for masonry. Cement-based paint may be used on nonglazed brick, stucco, cement, and cinder block. Ordinary house or trim paints may be used for the finish coats on gutters, downspouts, and hardware or grilles. Porch-and-deck paint may be used on both concrete and wooden porches and steps.

CHOOSING COLORS

Color is mostly a matter of personal preference. Remember that light colors repel heat and dark tones absorb heat (Fig. 7-6). Chalking paints should be avoided where the chalking may discolor adjacent surfaces.

Fig. 7-5. A semi-transparent stain adds both color and grain to wood. (COURTESY OF E. A. NORD CO.)

Fig. 7-6. Darker stains hold up better to the Sun and weather. (COURTESY OF E. A. NORD CO.)

Paints are available in many colors and shades. Some are ready mixed. The dealer has to mix others by adding or combining different colors. Dealers usually carry color charts showing the different possibilities. Here are some points to remember when selecting your colors.

Light colors make a small room seem larger. Conversely, dark colors make an overly large room appear smaller. This rule can be effectively used for doors, windows, and skylights in order to seemingly enlarge or reduce spaces and areas within your home (Fig. 7-7). Ceilings appear lower when darker than the walls and higher when lighter than the walls.

Paint generally dries to a slightly different color or shade. For a preview of the final color, brush a sample swatch of the paint on a piece of clean, white blotting paper. The blotting paper will immediately absorb the wet gloss. The color on the paper will be about the color of the paint when it dries on the wall.

Colors often change under artificial lighting. The type of artificial lighting also can make a difference. Incandescent lighting casts a warm,

Fig. 7-7. Dark stains offer accent to light walls and can serve to "frame" views. (COURTESY OF E. A. NORD CO.)

yellow glow. On the other hand, fluorescent lighting usually gives off a cooler, blue hue unless a warm white fluorescent tube is used.

Remember that most paint stores use fluorescent lighting. Consequently, a color that looks one shade in the paint store may look another shade when you get it home. Adjacent colors also affect the appearance. See Fig. 7-8.

ESTIMATING QUANTITY

For large jobs, paint is usually bought by the gallon. Paint for trim, such as door and window frames, is often purchased by the quart or even pint. The label usually indicates the number of square feet the paint in

Fig. 7-8. Wallpaper can complement the solid colors of doors and windows. (COURTESY OF MARVIN WINDOWS)

the container will cover when applied as directed. To determine the amount you need:

- Measure the height and width of the area you plan to paint. Multiply the two measurements together.
- Subtract from this figure any area you won't be painting, such as glass or metal.
- Divide the figure obtained into the number of square feet the paint container will cover. Multiply that figure by the number of coats to be applied. This will determine the amount of paint needed.

A door that measures 3 feet by $6^1/_2$ feet contains $19^1/_2$-square feet of surface. An $8^1/_2$ by $8^1/_2$-inch glass panel in the door won't be painted, so it is subtracted. The total is 19 square feet. If you plan to paint both sides of the door with two coats each, multiply 19 by four and you get 76. Allowing 4 square feet for the door edges, you need 80 square feet of coverage. This figure can then be used to purchase the appropriate amount of paint for your door.

Extra paint may be required to cover old colors if there is much change involved, such as a light color over a dark one or over a design. It's best to overestimate the amount of paint needed to avoid the risk of having to buy a small second batch later that might not exactly match the original batch. You should have extra paint on hand for later touch-up.

HOW TO PAINT

Read the paint can label carefully before starting. The label will contain general application instructions, as well as any instructions and directions for applying the specific paint. It will also give drying requirements.

For speed and convenience, homeowners usually prefer to use a roller on walls, ceilings, and other large surfaces, and a brush for trim, woodwork, corners, along edges, and in other places a roller can't reach. Rectangular applicators also are available that offer convenience for both large and small applications. Specially-shaped rollers and other applicators are available for painting woodwork, corners, edges, and other close places. Some may work fine; others may not work so well. A small brush may still be best for doors, windows, and skylights.

Remember that different kinds of brushes and rollers are recommended for different paints. The characteristics of the bristles affect how well paint is transferred to the painting surface. Your paint dealer should be able to furnish sound advice on what kind of brush or roller you'll need.

Indoor spray painting is not generally done by the homeowner, except for small jobs using pressurized cans of paint. Some homeowners use spray paint on door and window trim that is placed across sawhorses in the garage or outside before installation. On outside jobs, spraying is often the fastest method for large areas, but it is not practical for trim work.

A stepladder, protective coverings that guard against splashes and spillage on the wrong surfaces, and wiping rags are other items needed for painting.

WHEN TO PAINT

For best results with either oil-based or latex paint, and for an easier and better paint job, paint when the weather is mild and dry. The less humidity in the air, the quicker the paint will dry. Never apply an oil-based paint when the temperature is below 40 degrees Fahrenheit. Freezing temperatures should be avoided with any paint. Temperatures above 90 degrees Fahrenheit are not only uncomfortable to the painter, but they may cause the paint to dry too quickly. Consult the label for temperature limitations.

Start any outside painting after the morning dew has evaporated. Stop painting outside in the late afternoon or early evening or on cool fall days. This is more important with latex paint than with oil-based paint.

Paint surfaces after they have been exposed to the Sun and are in the shade. A good rule for exterior painting is to follow the Sun around the house. Painting in sunlight will cause the paint to dry more quickly, especially in hot weather. This may cause brush lap marks to appear in the freshly painted surface.

Don't paint in windy or dusty weather or when insects may get caught in the paint. Insects are usually the biggest problem during fall evenings. Don't try to remove them from wet paint. Brush them off after the paint dries.

HOW MANY COATS?

Three coats of paint are often recommended for new wooden surfaces—one primer and two finish coats. A two-coat system will last only about half as long as a three-coat system.

On old paint surfaces that are in good condition, one topcoat may be sufficient. If the paint is very thin, apply two topcoats, especially on outside surface areas that are exposed to weather or on any surface exposed to heavy use.

On bare surfaces or surfaces with very little paint left on them, apply a primer and two topcoats. Remove heavy chalk before repainting, especially when repainting with latex.

Allow the primer coat to dry according to the manufacturer's label instructions. Allow a longer drying time in humid weather. Apply the finish coats as soon as the primer has dried sufficiently. Allow about 48-hours drying time between oil-based finish coats. Two coats of latex paint may be applied in one day. If you must wait a month or more, clean the surface thoroughly before applying the topcoats.

On metal surfaces, prime both new metal and old metal from which the paint has been removed. Good primers usually contain zinc dust, red lead, zinc yellow, or some rust-inhibiting pigment as one of the ingredients. After the primer has dried sufficiently, apply one or two finish coats of paint.

PAINTING SAFETY

Never paint in a completely closed room, nor in one where there is an open flame. Solvent paints give off fumes that can be flammable and dangerous to breathe. Good cross ventilation helps to remove fumes and odors, and it can shorten paint drying time. Some fumes can be especially harmful to infants, children, and pets. Avoid sleeping in rooms with freshly painted finishes until the fumes subside.

Use a sturdy stepladder or other support when painting high places. Be sure the ladder is positioned firmly, both on the ground and against the wall. Set the foot of the ladder away from the wall one-fourth the distance of the height to be climbed. If you use scaffolding, make sure it is secure.

Always lean toward the ladder when painting. Keep one hand free and ready to grab the ladder. Don't over reach when painting. A good rule is to not let your belt buckle extend beyond the side rails.

When you finish painting, put used rags in a covered metal can. If they are left laying around, the oily rags could catch fire by spontaneous combustion. Store paint in a safe, ventilated place where children and

Fig. 7-9. The first step in preparing a door or other wood surface for finishing is to sand the entire surface with extra fine sandpaper. (COURTESY OF FIR & HEMLOCK DOOR ASSOCIATION)

pets cannot get to it. Keep paint and oily rags well away from furnaces or other sources of ignition that might cause an explosion.

PAINTING DOORS

Wooden panel doors should be finished after they have been fitted and hung. Remove the door from the hinges and place it in a dry area. Avoid finishing immediately after a rain storm or during periods of higher than average humidity. The door itself must be dry. Sand the entire surface with extra fine sandpaper (Fig. 7-9) and/or steel wool (Fig. 7-10) to remove marks, fingerprints, and stamps, and to clean off old, loose paint. Grease and oily stains can be removed with mineral spirits. Don't use water or caustic or abrasive cleaners. Clean the door thoroughly with a cloth to remove dust.

To obtain a quality stain or clear finish, use an oil-based sealer manufactured for exterior use such as finishing exterior doors (Fig. 7-11).

Fig. 7-10. Steel wool can also be used to sand carved wood or crevices. (COURTESY OF FIR & HEMLOCK DOOR ASSOCIATION)

Fig. 7-11. Your first coat should be an oil-based sealer manufactured for exterior use, such as finishing exterior doors. (COURTESY OF FIR & HEMLOCK DOOR ASSOCIATION)

Don't use lacquer-based or latex-based sealers. Sand lightly after the sealer has dried. If the door is to have weatherstripping, apply two coats of sealer to the edges before the weatherstripping is applied.

If a stained effect is desired, apply one or two coats of semi-transparent stain. Let it stand and wipe as needed to achieve the desired color (Fig. 7-12). Do not apply the stain before sealing as the wood will not accept the stain evenly.

Apply at least two topcoats of an exterior oil-based clear finish (Fig. 7-13). Marine quality varnishes and polyurethane finishes do a superior job as topcoats on exterior doors.

To obtain a quality painted finish, first use a good quality oil-based primer manufactured for exterior use. Sand lightly when dry. The second and third coats are color coats and may be either oil-based or latex-based exterior paints.

Fig. 7-12. Apply one or two coats of stain. Let it stand and wipe as needed to achieve the desired color. (COURTESY OF FIR & HEMLOCK DOOR ASSOCIATION)

Use sealers, primers, stains, and finish coatings from the same manufacturer, if possible, to ensure compatibility. Follow the manufacturer's instructions and consult your paint dealer.

Use sealer, primer, clear finishes, and paint liberally to fill in and bridge all voids in the joints between wooden sections and between the wood and any glass or insets in the door.

Sand lightly between coats of sealer, stain, and clear finishes. Never use lacquer-based stains or finishes on wooden panel doors. Nor should lacquer thinner be used to clean acrylic glazed doors.

PAINTING WINDOWS

Paint the wood dividing the window glass first (Fig. 7-14). Then paint the frame, trim, sill, and apron (Fig. 7-15).

Shutters and storm sashes are easier to paint if they are removed from the house and laid flat on supports. Clean off dust and dirt before painting them. Shrubbery may need to be covered with drop cloths.

Fig. 7-13. The final step is to apply at least two topcoats of an exterior oil-based clear finish. (COURTESY OF FIR & HEMLOCK DOOR ASSOCIATION)

Some people prefer to paint the windows after the walls have been completed. Others prefer the opposite. Be sure that whichever is painted first is completely dry before you paint the other.

Windows are easier to paint and to clean afterward if the glass is masked. One simple way to protect the glass is to cover it with a piece of wet newspaper. The moisture will paste the newspaper to the glass and also prevent paint from soaking into the absorbent paper. When you strip the paper from the glass after painting, the paint will come with it. Another method is to wipe a light layer of petroleum jelly around the edges of the glass with your finger. After the paint has dried, the jelly and paint can be cleaned away with any ordinary glass-cleaning compound.

Both masking tape and liquid masking are available at hardware and paint stores. Masking tape can be applied around all edges of the glass. It should border all wooden areas to be painted. When the paint is dry to the touch, remove the masking tape. If you wait too long, the dried paint

Fig. 7-14. Window trim and casing before painting. (COURTESY OF WEBB MANUFACTUR-ING INC.)

may crack upon removal of the tape and cause damage to the new paint job.

You need not apply masking. Paint smeared on the glass may be removed with a single-edged razor blade or other suitable scraper. After the paint is set but before it hardens, cut through the paint where the glass meets the wood. Starting at one corner, carefully scrape up a section of the paint and slowly lift it off the glass. If this strip of paint breaks, again carefully peel up a section large enough to grasp with your

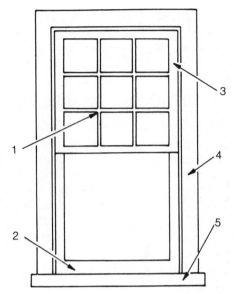

Fig. 7-15. Paint windows in this order: (1) mullions, (2) horizontal of sash, (3) verticals of sash, (4) verticals of frame, (5) horizontal frame and sill.

fingers and continue to carefully lift it away from the glass. Other drips or splatters of paint inadvertently applied to the glass may be easily scraped off at the same time.

Small rollers and pads are handy for painting the wood around windows.

PAINTING SKYLIGHTS AND SOLARIUMS

Painting skylight frames is much like painting any window frame. It's easier because there is less unfinished wood or metal in contact with the glass or plastic, so you have less masking and detail work. In another way, though, skylight painting is more difficult as it usually involves working on scaffolding or large ladders and platforms.

Skylight frames are often painted prior to installation or immediately afterward while the scaffold is still in place. Skylight frames usually can justify a higher quality paint and more coats than other surfaces in order to reduce the necessity of frequent repainting. As with other barriers, talk with your paint dealer to find out which paint and method is best for your application.

CLEANUP

After each job, replace the can lid. Make sure it is on tight. Brushes, rollers, and other equipment should be cleaned as soon after use as possible.

Equipment used to apply oil-based paint may be a little harder to clean. Soak brushes in turpentine or paint thinner long enough to loosen the paint. Work the bristles against the bottom of the container to release the paint. To release paint in the center of the brush, squeeze or work the bristles between the thumb and forefinger. Rinse the brush in the turpentine or thinner again and, if necessary, wash it in mild soapsuds. Rinse in clear water.

SOLVING PAINTING PROBLEMS

Some paint failures can be avoided by simply following the directions on the paint can label carefully. Some of the new paints and finishes are guaranteed against specific failures, if applied according to directions.

Excessive wetting of the paint from behind or from the front will cause blistering, peeling, and discoloration. Rain water, melted snow behind ice dams, or condensed water vapor may be getting in behind the paint. This problem can often be corrected before painting. Some searching may be required to detect the source. Check for leaks in roofs and sidewalls. Is the cause related to a damp basement? Are insulation, vapor barriers, and ventilation adequate? Make sure that moisture from appliances such as a clothes dryer is vented outside. Check for leaky plumbing.

To solve the problem, remove all loose paint. Apply a water-repellent preservative to joints that show damage. Allow the preservative coating to dry for two days or as directed on the container label. Prime the bare surfaces and repaint using a blister-resistant paint.

Cross-grain cracking may result if you paint too frequently with an oil-based paint. The thick paint coating becomes too hard to accommodate the constant expansion and contraction of the wood and eventually cracks.

To prevent cross-grain cracking, repaint only when necessary. Remove the paint down to the bare wood and prime the wood properly before repainting.

Mildew may occur where continuously warm and damp conditions prevail. If possible, correct moisture conditions that promote mildew. Use mildew-resistant paint or add a mildew-resistant compound to the paint. Thoroughly remove all signs of mildew before repainting. To remove mildew, mix 1 quart of household bleach and 3 quarts of warm water. Scrub the mildewed surface thoroughly with this solution. Give the surface a thorough rinsing with fresh water. Be sure to wash your hands and arms well when you are through.

Never mix bleach with any cleaning product that contains ammonia. The combination produces a lethal gas that has killed several people.

8

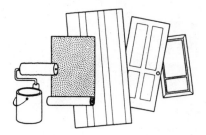

Increasing Energy Efficiency

BECAUSE OF THE NATIONAL CONCERN ABOUT THE ENERGY CRISES AND HIGH heating bills, people are increasingly interested in how they can weatherize their homes and increase energy efficiency. The first place to start is with barriers: doors, windows, and skylights (Fig. 8-1).

THERMAL INSULATION

Most materials used in houses have some insulating value. Even airspaces between studs resist the passage of heat. When these stud spaces are filled or partially filled with a material highly resistant to heat transmission, namely thermal insulation, the stud space has many times the insulating value of the air alone.

The inflow of heat through outside walls and roofs in hot weather or its outflow during cold weather will have important effects on the comfort of the occupants and the cost of needed heating or cooling. While the wood in doors, windows, skylights, and walls provides good insulation, commercial insulating materials are usually incorporated into air pockets around studs and barriers to increase their resistance to heat passage.

The average winter low-temperature zones of the United States are shown in Fig. 8-2. The data are used to determine the size of the required heating plant, after calculating heat loss. This information is also useful when selecting the amount of insulation for barriers, walls, ceilings, and floors.

Fig. 8-1. Energy efficient doors and windows can greatly increase a home's comfort and efficiency.

INSULATING MATERIALS

Commercial insulation is manufactured in many forms and types, each with advantages for specific uses. Materials commonly used for insulation can be broken into these classifications: flexible insulation (blanket and batt), loose-fill insulation, reflective insulation, rigid insulation (structural and nonstructural), and miscellaneous types.

The thermal properties of most building materials are known. The rate of heat flow or coefficient of transmission for most combinations of construction can be calculated. This coefficient, or U value, is a measure of heat transmission between air on the warm side and air on the cold side of the construction unit. The insulating value of the wall or barrier will vary with different types of construction, with the materials used in construction, and with different types and thicknesses of insulation. Comparisons of U values may be made and used to evaluate different combinations of materials and insulation based on overall heat loss, potential fuel savings, the influence on comfort, and installation costs.

Air spaces add to the total resistance of a wall section to heat transmission, but an airspace is not as effective as a similar space filled with an insulating material. Great importance is frequently given to dead-air spaces regarding a wall section. The air is never dead in cells where there are temperature differences on opposite sides of the space because the

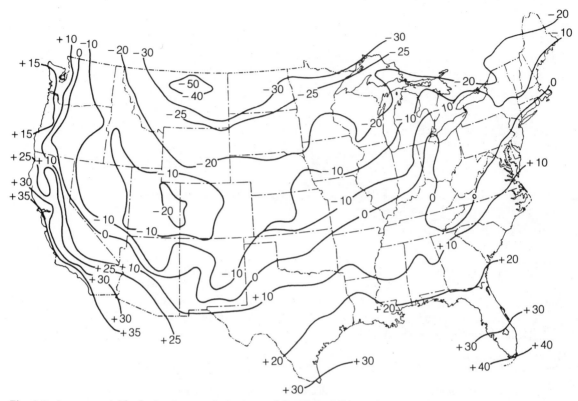

Fig. 8-2. Average outside design temperature zones of the United States.

difference in temperature causes convection currents. Exterior doors usually have a solid wood core because it is a good insulator. Many interior doors do not need an insulating value and are hollow core.

Flexible Insulation

Flexible insulation is most commonly used to insulate doors and windows. It is manufactured in two types, blanket and batt. Blanket insulation (Fig. 8-3) is furnished in rolls or packages in widths suited to 18- and 24-inch stud and joist spacing. Usual thicknesses are $1\frac{1}{2}$, 2, and 3 inches. The body of the blanket is made of felted mats of mineral or vegetable fibers such as rock or glass wood, wood fiber, and cotton. Organic insulations are treated to make them resistant to fire, decay, insects, and vermin. Most blanket insulation is covered with paper or other sheet material and has tabs on the sides for fastening to studs or joists. One covering sheet serves as a vapor barrier to resist the movement of water vapor. It should always face the warm side of the wall. Aluminum foil, asphalt, or plastic-laminated paper are commonly used as barrier materials.

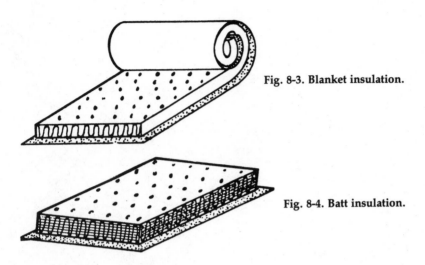

Fig. 8-3. Blanket insulation.

Fig. 8-4. Batt insulation.

Batt insulation (Fig. 8-4) is also made of fibrous material preformed to thicknesses of 4 and 6 inches for 18- and 24-inch joist spacing. It is supplied with or without a vapor barrier. One friction type of fibrous batt is supplied without a covering and is designed to remain in place without the usual fastening methods.

Loose-Fill Insulation

Loose-fill insulation (Fig. 8-5) is usually composed of materials that are used in bulk form. It is supplied in bags or bales, and placed by pouring, blowing, or packing by hand. This includes rock or glass wool, wood fibers, shredded redwood bark, cork, wood pulp products, vermiculite, sawdust, and shavings.

While loose-fill insulation is normally not directly installed around doors and windows, it is used between first-floor ceiling joists in unheated attics and around flat-roof skylights. Loose-fill insulation is sometimes blown into walls and around barriers that were previously installed without insulation.

Reflective Insulation

Most materials reflect some radiant heat, and some materials do so to a very high degree. Materials high in reflective properties include alumi-

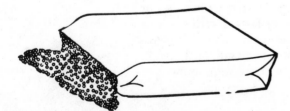

Fig. 8-5. Fill insulation.

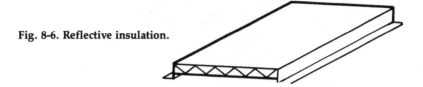

Fig. 8-6. Reflective insulation.

num foil, sheet metal with tin coating, and paper products coated with a reflective oxide. Such materials can be used in enclosed stud spaces, attics, and similar locations to retard heat transfer by radiation. These reflective insulations are effective only when used where the reflective surface faces an airspace at least $3/4$ inch or more deep. Foil-type reflective insulation is sometimes applied to blankets and to the stud-surface side of gypsum lath. Metal foil suitably mounted on some supporting base makes an excellent barrier. The type of reflective insulation shown in Fig. 8-6 includes reflective surfaces and airspaces between the outer sheets.

Rigid Insulation

Rigid insulation is usually a fiberboard material manufactured in sheet and other forms (Fig. 8-7). Rigid insulations are also made from inorganic fiber and glass fiber, though they are not commonly used in this form in a house. Structural insulating boards, in densities ranging from 15-31 lbs. per cu. foot, are fabricated into building boards, roof decking, sheathing, and wallboard. While they have moderately good insulating properties, their primary purpose is structural.

In house construction, the most common forms of rigid insulation are sheathing and decorative coverings in sheets or tile squares. Sheathing board is made in thicknesses of $1/2$ and $25/32$ inch. It is coated or impregnated with an asphalt compound to provide water resistance. Sheets are 2 by 8 feet for horizontal application and 4 by 8 feet or longer for vertical application.

Miscellaneous Insulation

Some insulations do not fit in the classifications previously described, such as insulation blankets made of multiple layers of corrugated paper. Other types, such as lightweight vermiculite and perlite aggregates, are sometimes used in plaster to reduce heat transmission.

Fig. 8-7. Rigid insulation.

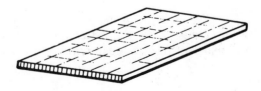

**Table 8-1. Thermal Conductivity
Values of Some Insulating Materials.**

Insulation Group		K range (conductivity)		
General	**Specific Type**			
Flexible		0.25	–	0.27
Fill	Standard materials	.28	–	.30
	Vermiculite	.45	–	.48
Reflective (2 sides)			(1)	
Rigid	Insulting fiberboard	.35	–	.36
	Sheathing fiberboard	.42	–	.55
Foam	Polystyrene	.19	–	.29
	Urethane	.15	–	.17
Wood	Low density	.60	–	.65

[1]Insulating value is equal to slightly more than 1 inch of flexible insulation. (Resistance R = 4.3)

Other materials are formed-in-place insulations, which include sprayed and plastic types. Sprayed insulation is usually inorganic fibrous material blown against a clean surface that has been primed with an adhesive coating. It is often left exposed for acoustical and insulating properties.

Expanded polystyrene and urethane plastic foams can be molded or foamed in place. Urethane insulation can also be applied by spraying. Polystyrene and urethane in board form can be obtained in thicknesses from $1/2$ to 2 inches. Foamed-in-place insulation is often used around barriers in older homes where insulation was not installed when the home was constructed.

Table 8-1 provides comparative insulating values for various materials. These are expressed as k values or heat conductivity and are defined as the amount of heat, in British thermal units (Btus), that will pass in 1 hour through 1 square foot of 1-inch thick material, per 1 degree Fahrenheit temperature difference between the faces of the material. Simply expressed, k represents heat loss; the lower this numerical value, the better the insulating quality.

Insulation is also rated on its resistance or R value, which is merely another expression of its insulating value. The R value is usually expressed as the total resistance of the wall, barrier, or thick insulating blanket or batt, whereas k is the rating per inch of thickness. For example, a k value of 1 inch of insulation is .025. The resistance or R value is $1/0.25$ or 4.0. If you have 3 inches thick of this insulation, the total R value is three times 4.0 or 12.0.

The U value is the overall heat loss value of all materials in the wall. The lower this value, the better the insulating value. For comparison with Table 8-1, the U value of window glass is:

Glass	U value
Single	1.13
Double	
Insulated, with ¹/₄-inch airspace	.61
Storm sash over single glazed window	.53

See Fig. 8-8 for heat gain comparisons.

WHERE TO INSULATE

Increasing the energy efficiency of doors, windows, and skylights is not confined to simply insulating these barriers. It also means making sure

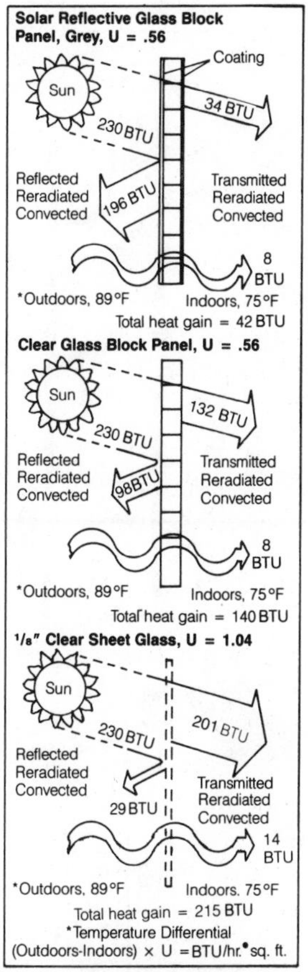

Fig. 8-8. Heat gain comparisons.

(1) Target Performance Criteria—all values are subject to manufacturing tolerances of +5%.

(2) For 12″ × 12″ blocks in panels, increase shading coefficients by 15% and decrease "U" value to .52.

(3) Shading coefficient is defined as the ratio of the solar heat gain through the glass block panel under a specific set of conditions to the solar heat gain through a single light of double-strength sheet glass under the same set of conditions.

that all elements of the home are efficiently insulated. To reduce heat loss from the house during cold weather, all barriers, walls, ceilings, roofs, and floors that separate heated spaces from unheated ones should be insulated (Figs. 8-9 through 8-11 and Table 8-2).

Insulation should be placed on all outside walls and the ceiling. In houses with unheated crawl spaces, it should be placed between the floor joists or around the wall perimeter. If a flexible type of insulation (blanket or batt) is used, it should be supported between joists by slats and a galvanized wire mesh or by a rigid board with the vapor barrier installed toward the subflooring. Press-fit or friction insulations fit tightly between joists and require only a small amount of support to hold them in place. Reflective insulation is often used for crawl spaces, but

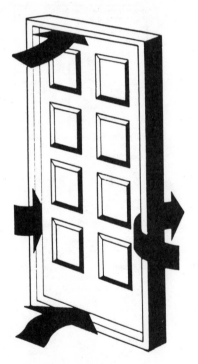

Fig. 8-9. Heat loss through doors.

Fig. 8-10. Heat loss through windows.

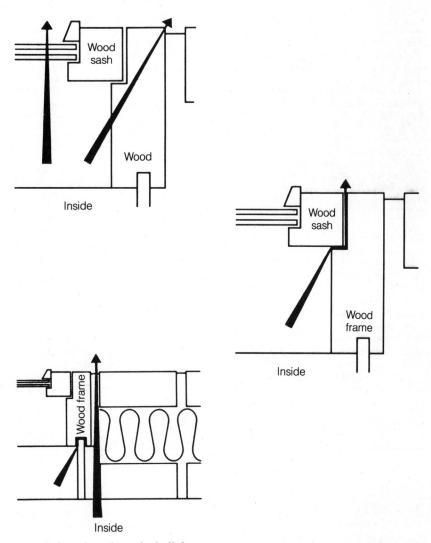

Fig. 8-11. Heat loss through skylights.

only one dead air space should be assumed in calculating heat loss when the crawl space is ventilated. A ground cover of roll roofing or plastic film such as polyethylene should be placed on the soil of the crawl space to decrease the moisture content of the space and of the wooden members.

The use of storm windows or insulated glass will greatly reduce heat loss. Almost twice as much heat loss occurs through a single glass pane as through a window glazed with insulated glass or protected by a storm sash (Figs. 8-12 and 8-13 and Table 8-3). Double glass panes will normally prevent surface condensation and frost from forming on inner glass surfaces in the winter. When excessive condensation persists, paint failures or even decay of the sash rail or other parts can occur.

Table 8-2. Calculating Heat Loss and Air Filtration.

Purpose

The purpose of the Door Insulating System Index (DISI) is to establish a standard method of rating the energy loss through a door assembly. The system was designed to provide a meaningful method of comparing the insulating efficiency of insulated steel doors and frames/weatherstripping as a unit. The Index is a single number that combines the heat losses due to both the transmission through the door and the infiltration of outside air around the perimeter (crack) of the door. Both must be combined to determine total heat loss.

Calculation

Heat losses resulting from transmission and air infiltration for a door assembly are computed as follows.

Heat Transmission

DISI Calculation

$$
\begin{aligned}
q_t &= \text{'U'} \times A \times 24 \times \Delta T° \\
&= .20 \times 20.0 \times 24 \times 25° \\
&= 2400 \text{ Btu per day}
\end{aligned}
$$

q_t	=	heat transfer (loss) due to transmission, Btus per day
U	=	.20 (ISDI-107, thermal performance standard for insulated steel door and weatherstripping frame assembly)
A	=	Door area for a 3'0" × 6'8" door, square feet
24	=	24 hours per day
ΔT	=	25° (inside temperature 65°—outside temperature 40°), Fahrenheit.

Air Infiltration

(resulting from a 25 mph wind pressure)

$$
\begin{aligned}
q_s &= .240 \times V \times \varrho \times 24 \times \Delta T° \\
&= .240 \times 580.2 \times .075 \times 24 \times 25 \\
&= 6266 \text{ Btu per day}
\end{aligned}
$$

q_s	=	Energy required to raise the temperature of air leaking into building from t_o to t_i, Btus per day
.240	=	Specific heat of air, Btus per pound per degree of Fahrenheit
V	=	Volume of air entering building, cubic feet per hour V = .50 × 19.34 × 60 min. = 580.2 .50 Maximum allowable infiltration rate, cubic feet per minute (ISDSI-101, Air Infiltration Performance Standard for Insulated Steel Door Systems) 19.34 Crackage, feet, around the perimeter of a 3'0" × 6' 8" door
ϱ	=	Density of standard air, 0.075 pounds per cubic foot
24	=	24 hours per day
$\Delta T°$	=	25° (inside temperature, 65°—outside temperature, 40°), Fahrenheit

Definitions

DISI Number
The total Btus lost for one day divided by 1,000.
Transmission
The amount of heat transmitted through the door slab.
Air Infiltration
The amount of air leakage that enters a building through cracks and interstices around the door.

INSTALLING INSULATION

Blanket insulation or batt insulation with a vapor barrier should be placed between framing members so that the tabs of the barrier lap the edge of the studs and the top and bottom plates. A hand stapler is commonly used to fasten the insulation and the barriers in place. For insulation without a barrier (press-fit or friction type), a plastic film vapor barrier such as 4-mil polyethylene is commonly used to envelop the entire exposed wall and ceiling. It covers the openings as well as window and door headers and edge studs.

Areas over door and window frames and along side and head jambs also require insulation (Fig. 8-14). Because these areas are filled with

Fig. 8-12. Four types of double- and triple-glazed windows. (COURTESY OF MARVIN WINDOWS)

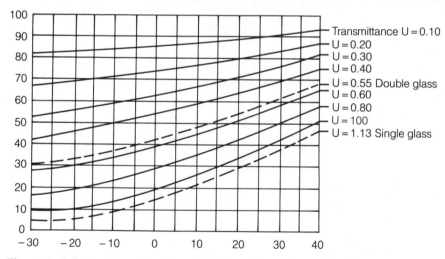

Fig. 8-13. Relationships of inside relative humidity and outside temperature for selecting glass.

small sections of insulation, a vapor barrier must be used around the opening and over the header above the openings. Enveloping the entire wall eliminates the need for this type of vapor barrier installation.

Fill insulation is commonly used in ceiling areas and is poured or blown into place. A vapor barrier should be used on the warm side—the

Table 8-3. Comparison of Yearly Heating Costs Using Various Glass and Sash Combinations.

	Minneapolis, Minn. (8400 degree days)	Burlington, Vt. (8200 degree days)	Green Bay, Wisc. (8000 degree days)	Sioux Falls, S.D. (7800 degree days)	Pittsfield, Mass. (7600 degree days)	Dubuque, Iowa (7400 degree days)	Binghamton, N.Y. (7200 degree days)	Lansing, Mich. (7000 degree days)	Albany, N.Y. (6800 degree days)	Chicago, Ill. (6600 degree days)	Champaign, Ill. (5800 degree days)	Bridgeport, Conn. (5600 degree days)	St. Joseph, Mo. (5400 degree days)	Wheeling, W. Va. (5200 degree days)	St. Louis, Mo. (5000 degree days)	Bloomington, Ind. (4800 degree days)	Baltimore, Md. (4600 degree days)
Gas Heat																	
Single glass & aluminum windows *	$828	$1,724	$688	$846	$1,165	$749	$819	$650	$991	$795	$584	$827	$596	$731	$521	$479	$740
Single glass & wooden windows	742	1,545	616	757	1,043	669	734	591	888	712	523	740	532	654	466	428	662
Double glass & aluminum windows **	634	1,320	527	647	892	570	627	505	759	608	447	633	456	559	399	365	566
Double glass & wooden windows (.5 cfm air infil.)	560	1,166	465	571	787	502	554	446	670	533	395	559	403	494	352	323	499
Double glass & wooden windows (.3 cfm air infil.)	493	1,026	409	503	693	440	487	392	589	472	347	492	354	435	310	284	440
Triple glass (IG & storm panel) & wooden windows (.3 cfm air infil.)	425	886	353	434	598	379	421	339	509	408	300	425	305	375	267	246	380
Oil Heat																	
Single glass & aluminum windows *	$1,999	$1,990	$1,854	$1,999	$1,928	$1,762	$1,748	$1,615	$1,892	$1,732	$1,380	$1,266	$1,570	$1,539	$1,492	$1,545	$1,351
Single glass & wooden windows	1,790	1,783	1,660	1,790	1,727	1,575	1,565	1,446	1,694	1,552	1,236	1,134	1,403	1,379	1,336	1,383	1,210
Double glass & aluminum windows **	1,530	1,524	1,419	1,530	1,476	1,342	1,338	1,236	1,448	1,326	1,057	969	1,202	1,178	1,142	1,183	1,034
Double glass & wooden windows (.5 cfm air infil.)	1,351	1,345	1,253	1,351	1,303	1,181	1,183	1,091	1,278	1,162	933	856	1,060	1,040	1,008	1,044	913
Double glass & wooden windows (.3 cfm air infil.)	1,188	1,184	1,103	1,188	1,146	1,036	1,040	960	1,125	1,029	821	753	933	915	887	918	804
Triple glass (IG & storm panel) & wooden windows (.3 cfm air infil.)	1,027	1,022	952	1,027	990	891	898	830	972	888	709	650	806	791	766	794	694
Electric Heat																	
Single glass & aluminum windows *	$1,112	$857	$1,310	$1,073	$871	$1,077	$1,672	$1,579	$1,668	$1,269	$727	$1,326	$1,253	$1,117	$828	$871	$1,050
Single glass & wooden windows	996	767	1,173	961	780	963	1,498	1,414	1,494	1,136	651	1,188	1,120	1,000	741	780	941
Double glass & aluminum windows **	851	656	1,003	821	667	820	1,280	1,209	1,277	970	556	1,015	959	855	634	667	804
Double glass & wooden windows (.5 cfm air infil.)	751	579	885	725	589	722	1,130	1,067	1,128	851	491	896	847	755	559	589	710
Double glass & wooden windows (.3 cfm air infil.)	661	509	779	638	518	633	995	939	992	753	432	789	745	664	492	518	625
Triple glass (IG & storm panel) & wooden windows (.3 cfm air infil.)	571	440	673	551	447	545	859	811	857	650	374	681	644	574	425	448	540

House Data Size: One story, 1,400 sq. ft. Gross outside wall area: 1,488 sq. ft. Ceiling area: 1,400 sq. ft. Windows and glazed doors: 378 sq. ft. Insulation: Ceilings R-32, walls R19. Floors over unheated basement. Two-inch insulation over ducts.

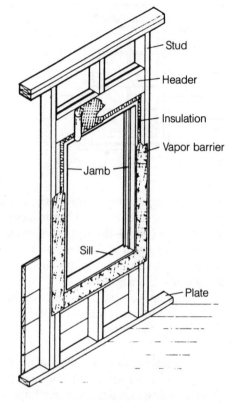

Stud

Header

Insulation

Vapor barrier

Jamb

Sill

Plate

**Fig. 8-14. Typical application of insu-
lation around windows.**

bottom side in the case of ceiling joists—before insulation is placed. A
leveling board can be used in many cases to give a constant insulation
thickness. Thick batt insulation is also used in ceiling areas. Batt and fill
insulation may be combined to obtain the desired thickness with the
vapor barrier against the backface of the ceiling finish. Ceiling insulation
6 inches or more thick greatly reduces heat loss in the winter and also
provides protection in the summer. Indirectly, this allows for the installation of lower efficiency, and thus less expensive, doors, windows, and
skylights.

CAULKING DOORS AND WINDOWS

Old and new homes often have many cracks and openings, especially
around windows and doors. These cracks are major sources of heat loss
from air leakage; warm air seeps out through cracks and is replaced by
cold, outdoor air. Annoying drafts are present near windows or doors
that need caulking and weatherstripping. Most doors fit loosely so they
will open and close smoothly. A crack of only 1/8 inch all around a standard front door is equivalent to a 4-inch by 8-inch opening—something
you would normally never tolerate in your home. In a properly insulated
home, air leakage can account for up to one-third of the heating costs.

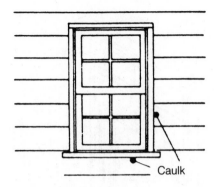

Fig. 8-15. Caulking around windows can reduce heat loss.

Caulk

Caulking is one of the easiest and most economical do-it-yourself projects to weatherproof a home against air leakage and, in turn, energy inefficiency (Fig. 8-15). Caulking should be used wherever two different materials or parts of a house meet at a stationary joint, such as around windows, doors, foundation sills, chimneys, water faucets, vents, electrical outlets, and pipes.

Caulking compounds are available in standardized 11-ounce cartridges that fit conventional caulking guns. There are several basic types of caulking compounds.

Elastomeric caulks. Silicones, polysulfides, and polyurethanes are examples. These are relatively easy to apply, give a neat bead, stick to most building surfaces, and are long-lasting. The caulks do not harden, will expand and contract slightly, and are in the higher price range. Some require primers on porous surfaces. Some accept paint; others do not. Follow instructions on the label.

Latex, butyl or polyvinyl-based caulks. These caulks are easy to apply, bond to most surfaces, are moderately durable, and are in the medium price range. Acrylic latex in premium grade is recommended for most applications. Better quality lines offer a performance guarantee; many lower-priced compounds provide no guarantee.

Oil- and resin-based caulks. These caulks are readily available. They bond to wood, masonry, and metal. They have a short life of two to three years and are in the lowest price range.

Filler. Oakum rope, caulking cotton, sponge rubber, fiberglass, or self-sticking caulking cord should be used to fill very wide cracks (3/8 inch or wider) before sealing with regular caulking. Insulation scraps may also be used for this purpose.

Lead-based caulk is not recommended because it is toxic. Many states ban its use.

To install caulking, first clean the area of chipping or flaking paint, dirt, and deteriorated caulk before applying the new caulk. Stuff filler in very wide cracks as needed. Lay a firm bead that overlaps both sides of the crack for a tight seal and firm adherence to substrate. Rough beads can be smoothed out or squeegeed off with a moistened fingertip.

TYPES OF WEATHERSTRIPPING

The use of weatherstripping helps prevent drafts and leaks around doors and windows (Fig. 8-16). The five types of weatherstripping are: perimeter or jamb weatherstripping that surrounds a door, under-door weatherstripping, thresholds, astrogals, and window weatherstripping.

Perimeter Weatherstripping

The three commonly used types of perimeter, jamb, or door weatherstripping are interlock, spring and cushion metal, and gasket.

The interlock type (Fig. 8-17), whether surface-mounted or concealed, consists of two metal members—one on the door and one on the opening—that interlock with one another. Very frequently it is rabbeted into the door and jamb to make it unobtrusive and to help protect it from

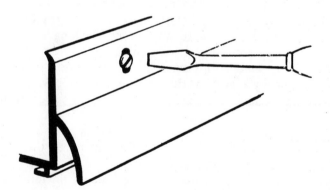

Fig. 8-16. Weatherstripping can greatly improve the energy efficiency of older doors and windows. (COURTESY OF PEMKO MANUFACTURING CO.)

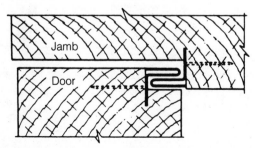

Fig. 8-17. Interlock weatherstripping. (COURTESY OF PEMKO MANUFACTURING CO.)

deformation. When attached in this manner, it is called concealed inter-lock.

On doors near areas where gravel abounds, interlock can cause problems. Small chunks of gravel may find their way underneath the interlock lip, usually on the threshold, and cause the interlocking hook to tear or the door to bind.

In cold areas, condensation and freezing may create a similar prob-lem all around exterior openings. To avoid this, spring metal may be used instead. Gasket weatherstripping is even better.

Unless there is a severe water problem, a plain interlock threshold should normally be used with interlock weatherstripping on the door. This combination is preferable to a waterproof interlock threshold because material may build up in the threshold trough. When there is a water problem, a waterproof interlock threshold with additional protec-tion from a rain drip is advised.

Cushion and Spring Metal Weatherstripping

These may be made of bronze, aluminum, or stainless steel. Alumi-num is cheaper, but it is weaker and may break as it comes in contact with other aluminum. Stainless steel has the virtues of aluminum with-out the drawbacks, but it is more costly than bronze.

Cushion weatherstripping is formed by folding a strip into the shape of a V so that one leg is shorter than the other. The long leg is attached to the door jamb. The door then closes against the shortest leg.

Spring-type weatherstripping (Fig. 8-18) consists of a ribbon of spring metal usually as wide as the door permits. This weatherstripping is mounted on the jamb with nails, metal screws, or drive pins in a posi-tion where the door will close against it. One edge is usually made with a slight crimp about 1/4 inch wide. When this edge is fastened to the jamb, the other portion of the strip is thrown out so the door closes against it with a slight pressure.

Cushion and spring weatherstripping function in much the same way. They are usually interchangeable. They give a good degree of draft

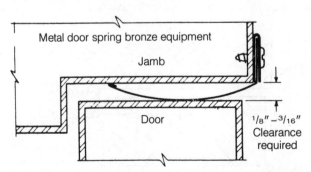

Fig. 8-18. Spring metal weatherstripping. (COURTESY OF PEMKO MANUFACTURING CO.)

control and may be used on exterior doors where condensation and freezing may make interlock impractical. This weatherstripping is frequently sold in the Midwest because of the freezing problem. It is often used in doors fabricated of hollow metal or other materials that do not permit the installation of concealed interlock.

Both spring and cushion weatherstripping may make a door a trifle harder to operate than normal and may cause a slight closing sound. When installing such weatherstripping, it may be difficult to make even contact because the stripping may develop a wave. Also, wind may cause the weatherstripping to produce an annoying hum. The weatherstripping can also be damaged and pulled out of shape, sometimes developing jagged edges.

The faults of spring and cushion weatherstripping are not extreme and are balanced by the virtues of being inexpensive and fairly effective. They are being used less frequently, however, because new gasket types are taking their place.

Gasket Weatherstripping

Gasket weatherstripping (Fig. 8-19) consists of an aluminum or bronze retainer strip, which holds a vinyl, rubber, or neoprene extrusion, a sponge or felt rubber strip, or plain felt or wool pile. Until the development of vinyl and neoprene gaskets, the use of this weatherstripping was subject to many drawbacks (Fig. 8-20). For example, felt or wool pile may become worn or misshaped. Rubber wore and aged so that it either became sticky or it dried out and cracked. Often the full effectiveness of the gasket was destroyed due to children or thoughtless persons picking it apart. Modern synthetic neoprene rubbers have overcome these drawbacks.

Unlike cushion or spring weatherstripping, it is almost impossible to derange gasket weatherstripping to the extent that it becomes ineffective, particularly when screw holes are slotted for adjustment.

Gasket weatherstripping is nearly always surface-applied, which means that it does not have to be routed into the door or jamb. The

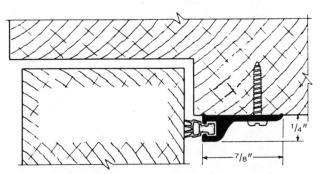

Fig. 8-19. Gasket weatherstripping. (COURTESY OF PEMKO MANUFACTURING CO.)

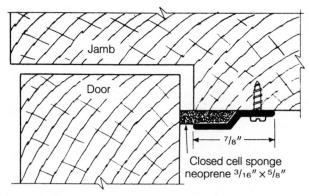

Fig. 8-20. Neoprene gasket weatherstripping. (COURTESY OF PEMKO MANUFACTURING CO.)

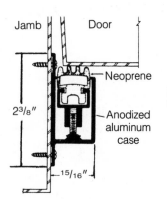

Fig. 8-21. Adjustable gasket weatherstripping. (COURTESY OF PEMKO MANUFACTURING CO.)

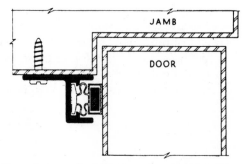

Fig. 8-22. Magnetic gasket weatherstripping. (COURTESY OF PEMKO MANUFACTURING CO.)

weatherstripping is quickly and easily installed, and is often adjustable (Figs. 8-21 through 8-27).

A type of gasket weatherstripping called the sweep is used to weatherstrip garage doors. It is designed to adequately cover large opening gaps and to fit against rough and uneven floors (Fig. 8-28). It is normally made of rubber, neoprene, or vinyl and is simple to install.

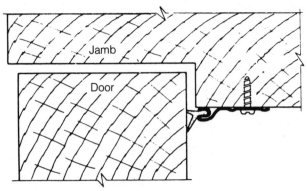

Fig. 8-23. Multiple ridge gasket weatherstripping. (COURTESY OF PEMKO MANUFACTUR-ING CO.)

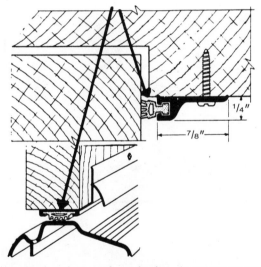

Fig. 8-24. Feather-edged gasket weatherstripping. (COURTESY OF PEMKO MANUFACTUR-ING CO.)

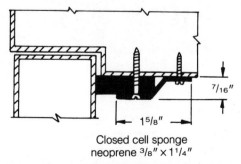

Closed cell sponge
neoprene $3/8'' \times 1 1/4''$

Fig. 8-25. Closed-cell sponge neoprene gasket weatherstripping. (COURTESY OF PEMKO MANUFACTURING CO.)

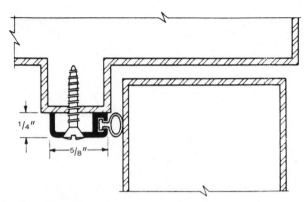

Fig. 8-26. Weatherstripping can be specially designed to fit unique applications such as this door with a small stop. (COURTESY OF PEMKO MANUFACTURING CO.)

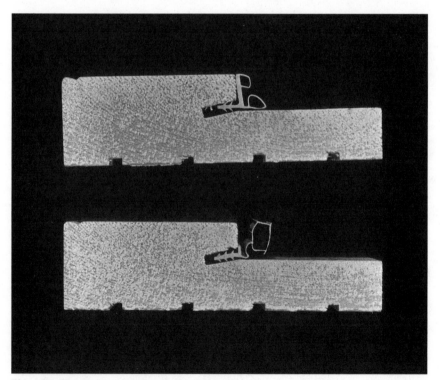

Fig. 8-27. Two types of gasket weatherstripping. (COURTESY OF PEASE INDUSTRIES, CO.)

Astrogals

An astrogal is the weatherstripping installed where double doors meet. There are basically two types of double doors and many types of astrogals. Single-acting doors only swing in one direction with one door locking first and the other closing against it. Double-acting doors swing in both directions.

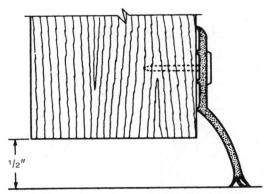

Fig. 8-28. Sweep gasket weatherstripping is popular for garage doors. (COURTESY OF PEMKO MANUFACTURING CO.)

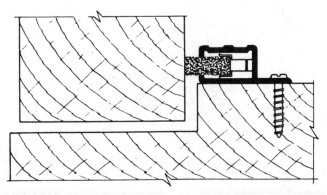

Fig. 8-29. Felt gasket weatherstripping. (COURTESY OF PEMKO MANUFACTURING CO.)

For single-acting double doors, there are many astrogals in wood, metal, wood pile, neoprene, vinyl, etc. Wool pile in a channel inset (Fig. 8-29) is effective and can be replaced. A pair of aluminum strips that hold hollow vinyl or neoprene insets can also be used (Fig. 8-30). One strip is attached to each door so that the inset hangs over the edge and presses against the inset of the other door. Cushion metal astrogals (Fig. 8-31) sometimes catch onto passing things. Heavy-duty spring metal is better if this type of weatherstripping must be used. Some plain metal or wooden astrogals, with or without a backing strip of neoprene, are augmented by cushion metal between the doors.

With double-acting doors, there is the added factor of wear as the two doors swing against one another. The best astrogals for this situation are ordinarily those that incorporate wool pile on one door (Fig. 8-32). There are excellent heavy-duty adjustable astrogals for either wooden or hollow metal double-acting doors (Figs. 8-33 and 8-34). These can be made to compensate for any change in the fit of the doors simply by adjusting some screws located on 10-inch centers.

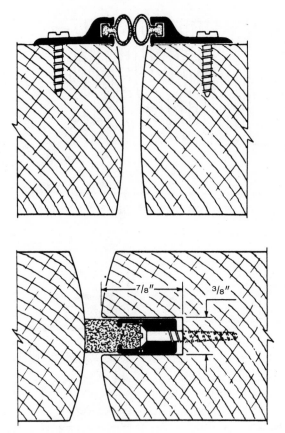

Fig. 8-30. Gasket weatherstripping for double-action doors. (COURTESY OF PEMKO MANUFACTURING CO.)

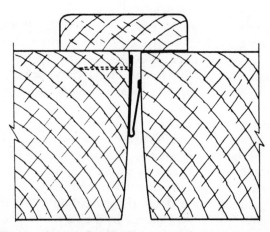

Fig. 8-31. Cushion metal astragal. (COURTESY OF PEMKO MANUFACTURING CO.)

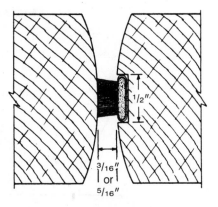

Fig. 8-32. To reduce gasket wear, some double-action doors use wood pile gaskets. (COURTESY OF PEMKO MANUFACTURING CO.)

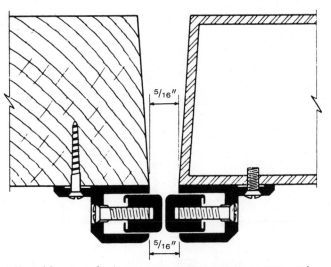

Fig. 8-33. Adjustable astragals. (COURTESY OF PEMKO MANUFACTURING CO.)

Fig. 8-34. Adjustable gasket astragals. (COURTESY OF PEMKO MANUFACTURING CO.)

The newly-designed weather seal security astrogal automatically seals and covers the gap between out-opening double doors (Fig. 8-35). This is important where security is required (Fig. 8-36).

Under-Door Weatherstripping

Under-door weatherstripping usually functions in conjunction with a threshold. There are many types of under-door weatherstripping

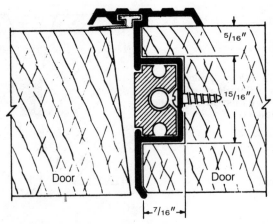

Fig. 8-35. Magnetic seal astragal. (COURTESY OF PEMKO MANUFACTURING CO.)

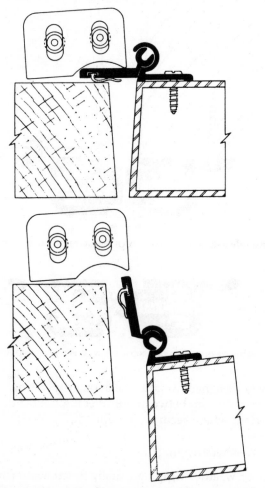

Fig. 8-36. Security astragal. (COURTESY OF PEMKO MANUFACTURING CO.)

including rain drip, spring metal, interlock, door sweep, door shoe, and automatic door bottom.

When no provision is made to seal the crack between the door and threshold on an exterior door, a rain drip (drip cap) may be attached to the outside of the door (Fig. 8-37). This is merely an eave-like strip that overhangs the bottom of the door and deflects the rain beyond the threshold.

Spring metal is sometimes used under doors. It creates a scraping feeling and sound. It is not recommended where there is a metal threshold.

Interlock under-door weatherstripping is similar to the interlock discussed under perimeter weatherstripping. An interlock lip (Fig. 8-38) on the threshold fits into an interlock hook fastened under the door. It can do an excellent job.

The door sweep is a simple type of surface-applied weatherstripping that attaches to the door bottom so that it contacts the threshold and seals out drafts, dust, and light (Fig. 8-39). Modern door sweeps are made of metal channel that holds flexible vinyl or neoprene sweeps. Older types may use felt or rubber. Some modern sweeps have slotted screw holes for adjustment purposes.

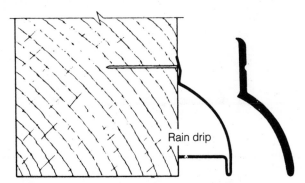

Rain drip

Fig. 8-37. Rain drip under-door weatherstripping. (COURTESY OF PEMKO MANUFACTURING CO.)

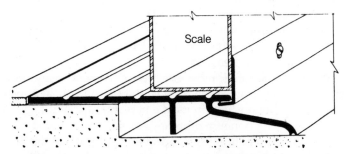

Scale

Fig. 8-38. Interlocking saddle under-door weatherstripping. (COURTESY OF PEMKO MANUFACTURING CO.)

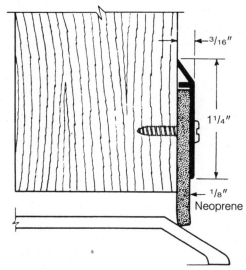

Fig. 8-39. Neoprene under-door sweep weatherstripping. (COURTESY OF PEMKO MANU-FACTURING CO.)

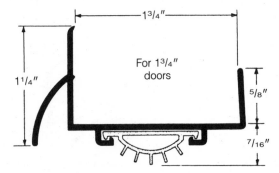

Fig. 8-40. Door shoe weatherstripping. (COURTESY OF PEMKO MANUFACTURING CO.)

The door shoe provides an excellent seal and a wiping action. It has become increasingly popular as an under-door weatherstrip. The door shoe (Fig. 8-40) consists of an aluminum extrusion fastened underneath the door, out of sight, and untouched by traffic—a problem encountered with the bubble seal threshold (Fig. 8-41). This threshold holds a vinyl or neoprene section that is both a bubble and a set of flexible fingers, which give it a multiple sealing action on top of the threshold. The door shoe is very simple to install and easy to adjust.

The most sophisticated, most effective, and most costly under-door seal is the automatic door bottom (Figs. 8-42 and 8-43). It consists of a metal frame that contains within itself a movable strip with a lower edge of felt or closed-cell sponge neoprene. Actualized by a rod protruding slightly from the door bottom, this movable strip drops to the floor when the door is closed and lifts when the door is opened. It provides excellent protection against dust, noise, drafts, and light.

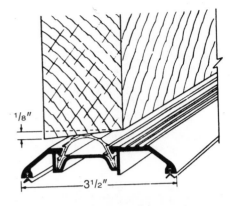

Fig. 8-41. Threshold with bubble seal. (COURTESY OF PEMKO MANUFACTURING CO.)

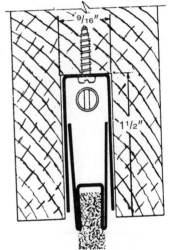

Fig. 8-42. Automatic door bottom. (COURTESY OF PEMKO MANUFACTURING CO.)

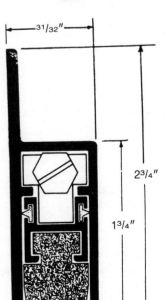

Fig. 8-43. Heavy-duty automatic door bottom. (COURTESY OF PEMKO MANUFACTURING CO.)

Thresholds

A threshold fills the necessary gap under a door (Figs. 8-44 and 8-45). This gap is needed to allow the door to swing freely. Without it, the door would have to be perfectly plumb in every direction and remain so, a condition which is practically impossible. Any settling of the building, warping of the door or jamb, or loosening of door butts would cause the door to scrape on the floor unless some gap is allowed under it. A threshold fills in most of this gap. It helps to keep out water, snow, dust, dirt, and some noise and light.

Fig. 8-44. Threshold with automatic door bottom. (COURTESY OF PEASE INDUSTRIES, INC.)

Fig. 8-45. Threshold details. (COURTESY OF PEASE INDUSTRIES, INC.)

Thresholds are available in wood, extruded aluminum, extruded brass, cast iron, and steel. They can be used with interlock weatherstripping on the door. Wooden or aluminum thresholds are considered satisfactory for light or ordinary traffic conditions, but for heavy traffic patterns the threshold should be of extruded brass, cast iron, or steel.

The most commonly used types of threshold are: saddle, interlock, gasket, and special. Saddle thresholds are plain thresholds that are used largely for interior doors and are intended to fill the gap under the door. There are two types: straight (Fig. 8-46), which can be either plain or fluted; and panic (Fig. 8-47), which are made for panic exit doors and incorporate a stop for the panic latch bolt to engage.

Interlock thresholds work in the same manner as interlocking weatherstripping (Fig. 8-48). They make excellent seals. The interlocking hook, however, can be damaged or forced out of adjustment (Fig. 8-49). This often happens when a piece of gravel gets into it. When the door is slammed, the hook is jimmied. This is less of a problem with the surface-applied hook because it can be fixed more easily. Interlock thresholds are divided into plain interlock and interlock with a water drain feature (Fig. 8-50).

A gasket threshold consists of a metal threshold with a vinyl bubble inset that runs its length underneath the door. The door exerts a slight

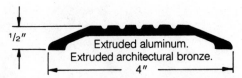

Fig. 8-46. Saddle threshold. (COURTESY OF PEMKO MANUFACTURING CO.)

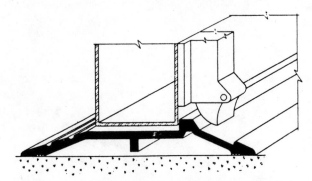

Fig. 8-47. Panic door threshold. (COURTESY OF PEMKO MANUFACTURING CO.)

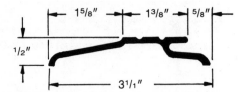

Fig. 8-48. Interlock threshold. (COURTESY OF PEMKO MANUFACTURING CO.)

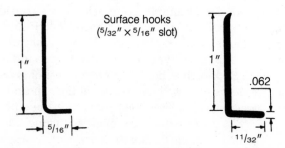

Fig. 8-49. Interlock surface hooks. (COURTESY OF PEMKO MANUFACTURING CO.)

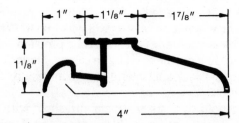

Fig. 8-50. Waterproof interlock threshold. (COURTESY OF PEMKO MANUFACTURING CO.)

pressure against this bubble to make a seal. These gaskets are subject to wear and pounding from traffic. Long before they wear through, however, they lose their shape and fail to perform properly. These gaskets are often impossible to replace because so many types were made—many by manufacturers that have since gone out of business.

Each year the variety of thresholds increases as designs are made to solve special problems including offset floors (Fig. 8-51), thin floors (Fig. 8-52), thick floors (Fig. 8-53), and other needs (Figs. 8-54 and 8-55).

WEATHERSTRIPPING AGAINST DRAFTS

In commercial and industrial buildings, as well as in homes, few things can be as annoying as drafts. When drafts are eliminated, colds and coughs tend to decrease. All exterior doors should be weatherstripped for draft control. Anything that keeps out drafts also eliminates the

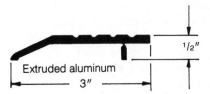

Fig. 8-51. Half threshold for offset floors. (COURTESY OF PEMKO MANUFACTURING CO.)

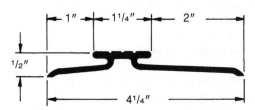

Fig. 8-52. Low silhouette saddle threshold. (COURTESY OF PEMKO MANUFACTURING CO.)

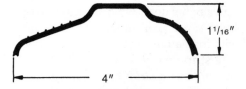

Fig. 8-53. High silhouette threshold. (COURTESY OF PEMKO MANUFACTURING CO.)

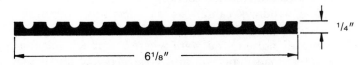

Fig. 8-54. Threshold expansion joint. (COURTESY OF PEMKO MANUFACTURING CO.)

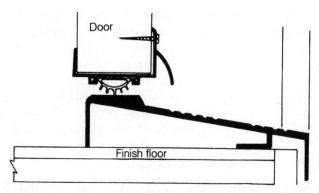

Fig. 8-55. Threshold/sill combination available with some prehung doors. (COURTESY OF PEMKO MANUFACTURING CO.)

entrance of dust and some noise. Under certain conditions, there also may be drafts around interior doors. All windows, especially in older buildings, should have good weatherstripping applied. Due to shrinkage through the years, wooden window frames may permit drafts. A rib-strip weatherstripping or one of the combinations of feather-edged vinyl and aluminum cover strips will eliminate this problem. For temporary purposes, polyurethane foam strips with pressure-sensitive backs may be used.

The three types of weatherstripping discussed under perimeter and window weatherstripping are effective in eliminating drafts. Some, however, are far more durable.

WEATHERSTRIPPING AGAINST NOISE

Soundproofing ideally should be included in the original plans of a building. Otherwise, inadequate doors may have to be replaced with insulated doors. For sound dampening, the placement of weatherstripping around any kind of door will help.

Although noise can be shut off around the perimeter of a door, it can easily come through a panel door, while a hollow door acts as a sounding board and transmits noise. For proper soundproofing, hollow doors should be filled with insulation, or a double set of doors should be used.

The best weatherstripping for soundproofing is the gasket type. It is quite effective for ordinary soundproofing purposes and is easily installed. Many doors that require soundproofing are interior doors. They don't require the protection of an interlocking threshold and are well served by an automatic door bottom. Door shoes are also effective.

Single-pane windows cannot be as effectively soundproofed as doors. Felt, wool pile, feather-edged vinyl, or neoprene sponge strips can reduce outside noise to the point where it is much less noticeable. Pressure-sensitive foam tape will also reduce noise, but it may need more frequent replacement. The new double-paned windows available in any size at low cost offer more effective soundproofing.

WEATHERSTRIPPING AGAINST DUST

A good weatherstripping could, in one year, save enough money in cleaning bills alone to pay for the entire cost of installing weatherstripping in one of the older types of buildings. So states a leading industrial and commercial weatherstripping firm.

Any type of weatherstripping helps reduce the dust problem because anything that eliminates drafts also keeps out dust and noise. The best choice is probably the gasket type.

Through the years, wooden windows shrink and permit dust and soot to enter around them. A rib-strip weatherstripping, one of the vinyl-aluminum combination strips, or even press-on foam tape will practically eliminate this nuisance.

WEATHERSTRIPPING AGAINST LEAKS

Most weatherstripping in good condition will prevent ordinary leaks around both windows and doors. Doors seldom leak anywhere but at the bottom. This water may originate along the jamb. When a door is directly exposed to driving rain or snow, a combination of two types of weatherstripping is frequently used. In the past, this has usually consisted of a mortised-in interlock plus a surface interlock. More recently, a combination of interlock and gasket weatherstripping has been used with success. At the door bottom, a combination of a rain drip on the outside plus a water-drain type of threshold is satisfactory. The combination seems to create an eddy under the door that prevents moisture from being blown underneath. A door shoe with an integral rain drip will also do the job. The threshold must be carefully caulked at the ends and along the back leg.

Double-hung windows for years have used interlock weatherstripping (a rib strip) that has proven quite effective against leaks.

The use of cushion metal weatherstripping for aluminum casement windows also helps prevent leaks. Some types snap into the flanges of the vent; others snap onto the frame.

The use of wool pile weatherstripping on sliding windows and sliding doors is also quite efficient. Although it is treated so as not to absorb water, some users claim that it may do so after long use or that it may become matted down, as sometimes happens around car windows. Vinyl-and-aluminum gasket weatherstripping is also available for sliding windows and doors.

SELECTING THE RIGHT WEATHERSTRIPPING

There are two basic recommendations made by experts in the selection of any weatherstripping. Modern weatherstripping should be permanent. Weatherstripping that depends on a rubbing action, such as spring metal and bubble thresholds, should not be used unless it is unavoidable.

A second feature to look for in any weatherstripping is adjustability. If it is completely unadjustable, it may soon lose its effectiveness. Ask an experienced builder, architect, weatherstripping contractor, or building materials dealer for help when choosing the appropriate weatherstripping package for your doors, windows, and skylight.

WEATHERSTRIPPING TOOLS

Most types of weatherstripping for doors can be installed by the inexperienced handyman. Generally, the following tools and supplies are needed to do a satisfactory job: hammer, measuring tape, screwdriver, knife or shears, tin snips, hand saw, hacksaw, plane, and appropriate nails, screws, and fasteners. Installing weatherstripping in windows and skylights will require most of these tools. Follow the safety rules in chapter 6.

Weatherstripping is available either by the running foot or in kit form for each barrier. In either case, first list all doors and windows, then measure each to find the total length of weatherstripping needed. Measure the total distance around the edges of moving parts. Be sure to allow for waste. If using weatherstripping in kit form, select the kit intended for your door or window type and size. Jalousie-type windows require a special weatherstripping—a clear vinyl channel that slips over the edge of each set of glass. Finding the correct size and shape can be difficult, but installation is quick and simple.

Glossary

apron—The flat member of the inside trim of a window that is placed against the wall immediately beneath the stool.

areaway—An open subsurface space adjacent to a building that is used to admit light or air or as a means of access to a basement.

astrogal—A molding attached to one of a pair of swinging doors against which the other door strikes.

backband—A simple molding sometimes used around the outer edge of plain rectangular casing as a decorative feature.

bearing wall—A wall that supports any vertical load in addition to its own weight.

blind nailing—Nailing in such a way that the nailheads are not visible on the face of the work. They are usually placed at the tongue of matched boards.

blind stop—A rectangular molding, usually $3/4$ by $1^3/8$ inches or more in width, that is used in the assembly of a window frame. It serves as a stop for storm and screen or combination windows and to resist air infiltration.

buck—Often used in reference to rough frame opening members. Door bucks used in reference to metal door frames.

butt joint—The junction where the ends of two timbers or other members meet in a square-cut joint.

cap—The upper member of a column, pilaster, door cornice, molding, and the like.

casement frames and sash—Frames of wood or metal that enclose part or all of the sash, which may be opened by hinges affixed to the vertical edges.

casing—Molding of various widths and thicknesses that is used to trim door and window openings at the jambs.

checking—Fissures that appear with age in many exterior paint coatings, at first superficial, but which in time may penetrate entirely through the coating.

condensation—Beads or drops of water, and frequently frost in extremely cold weather, that accumulate on the inside of the exterior covering of a building when warm, moisture-laden air from the interior reaches a point where the temperature permits the air to sustain the moisture it holds. Use of louvers or attic ventilators will reduce moisture condensation in attics. A vapor barrier under the gypsum lath or drywall on exposed walls will reduce condensation in them.

crawl space—A shallow space below the living quarters of a house without a basement. It is normally enclosed by the foundation wall.

dado—A rectangular groove across the width of a board or plank. In interior decoration, a special type of wall treatment.

door jamb, interior—The surrounding case into which and out of which a door closes and opens. It consists of two upright pieces called side jambs and a horizontal head jamb.

dormer—An opening in a sloping roof, the framing of which projects out to form a vertical wall suitable for windows or other openings.

drip cap—A molding placed on the exterior top side of a door or window frame to cause water to drip beyond the outside of the frame.

fire-stop—A solid, tight closure of a concealed space placed to prevent the spread of fire and smoke through such a space. In a frame wall, this will usually consist of 2 by 4 cross blocking between studs.

framing, balloon—A system of framing a building in which all vertical structural elements of the bearing walls and all partitions consist of single pieces extending from the top of the foundation sill plate to the roof plate and to which all floor joists are fastened.

framing, platform—A system of framing a building in which floor joists of each story are below or on the foundation sill for the first story, and the bearing walls and partitions rest on the subfloor of each story.

grain, edge (vertical)—Edge-grain lumber has been sawed parallel to the pith of the log and approximately at right angles to the growth rings; i.e., the rings form an angle of 45 degrees or more with the surface of the piece.

grain, flat—Flat-grain lumber has been sawed parallel to the pith of the log and approximately tangent to the growth rings; i.e., the rings form an angle of less than 45 degrees with the surface of the piece.

grain, quartersawed—Another term for edge grain.

header—A beam placed perpendicular to joists and to which joists are nailed in framing for chimney, stairway, doors, or windows. Also, a wooden lintel.

I beam—A steel beam with a cross section resembling the letter I. It is used for long spans as basement beams or over wide wall openings, such as a double garage door, when wall and roof loads are imposed on the opening.

insulation, thermal—Any material high in resistance to heat transmission that, when placed in the walls, ceiling, or floors of a structure, will reduce the rate of heat flow.

jamb—The side and head lining of a doorway, window, or other opening.

kiln-dried lumber—Lumber that has been kiln-dried often to a moisture content of 6 to 12%. Common varieties of softwood lumber, such as framing lumber, are dried to a somewhat higher moisture content.

lumber, boards—Yard lumber less than 2 inches thick and 2 inches or more wide.

lumber, dimension—Yard lumber from 2 inches to, but not including, 5 inches thick and 2 inches or more wide. It includes joists, rafters, studs, planks, and small timbers.

lumber, dressed size—The dimension of lumber after shrinking from green dimension and after machining to size or pattern.

lumber, matched—Lumber that is dressed and shaped on one edge in a grooved pattern and on the other in a tongued pattern.

lumber, shiplap—Lumber that is edge-dressed to make a close rabbeted or lapped joint.

millwork—Generally, all building materials made of finished wood and manufactured in millwork plants and planing mills are known as millwork. Such items as inside and outside doors, window and door frames, blinks, porchwork, mantels, panelwork, stairways, moldings, and interior trim are included. Millwork normally does not include flooring, ceilings, or siding.

miter joint—The joint of two pieces at an angle that bisects the joining angle. For example, the miter joint at the side and head casing at a door opening is made at a 45-degree angle.

moisture content of wood—Weight of the water contained in the wood, usually expressed as a percentage of the weight of the oven-dried wood.

molding—A wooden strip that has a curved or projecting surface and is used for decorative purpose.

mullion—Vertical bar or divider in the frame between windows, doors, and other openings.

muntin—A small member that divides the glass or openings of sash or doors.

on center—The measurement of spacing for studs, rafters, joists, and the like in a building from the center of one member to the center of the next.

parting stop or strip—A small wooden piece used in the side and head jambs of double-hung windows to separate the upper and lower sashes.

preservative—Any substance that, for a reasonable length of time, will prevent the action of wood-destroying fungi, borers of various kinds, and similar destructive agents when the wood has been properly coated or impregnated with it.

quarter-round—A small molding that has the cross section of a quarter circle.

rabbet—A rectangular longitudinal groove that is cut in the corner edge of a board or plank.

rail—The cross members of panel doors or of a sash. Also, the upper and lower members of a balustrade or staircase that extends from one vertical support, such as a post, to another.

sash—A single light frame that contains one or more lights of glass.

sash balance—A device that is usually operated by a spring or tensioned weatherstripping designed to counterbalance a double-hung window sash.

sill—The member forming the lower side of an opening as a doorsill, windowsill, etc.

stile—An upright framing member in a panel door.

trim—The finish materials in a building, such as moldings, that are applied around openings (window trim, door trim) or at the floor and ceiling of rooms (baseboard, cornice, and other moldings).

truss—A frame or jointed structure that is designed to act as a beam or long span, while each member is usually subjected to longitudinal stress only, either tension or compression.

vapor barrier — Material used to retard the movement of water vapor through walls and to prevent condensation in walls. It usually has a perm value of less than 1.0 and is applied separately over the warm side of exposed walls or as a part of batt or blanket insulation.

water-repellent preservative—A liquid designed to penetrate into wood and impart water repellency and a moderate preservative protection. It is used for millwork, such as sashes and frames, and is usually applied by dipping.

Index